LENNON, THE MOBSTER & the LAWYER

THE UNTOLD STORY

by

JAY BERGEN

FOREWORD by BOB GRUEN

**DEVAULT
GRAVES
BOOKS**

THE GREAT MUSIC BOOK SERIES

Library of Congress Cataloging-in-Publishing Data

Bergen, James
Lennon, the Mobster, and the Lawyer: The Untold Story

Library of Congress Control Number: 2021953348

Print Edition ISBN: 978-1-942531-42-5
E-book Edition ISBN: 978-1-942531-43-2

1. John Lennon—Music—*Rock 'n' Roll* album
2. John Lennon—Morris Levy—Lawsuit
3. John Lennon—countersuit--royalties
4. Morris Levy—*Roots* album

PR 6062 E6 L 2021   782.4216609 Be

10 9 8 7 6 5 4 3 2 1
First Edition

Cover design: Martina Voriskova
Layout design: Nancy Apple
Cover photograph and all other photographs
except where noted: Bob Gruen

**DEVAULT
GRAVES
BOOKS**
Devault Graves Books, Memphis

"I'm going to tell you something. John Lennon testified of course. . . . I certainly grew to respect [him] and the witnesses he called to show the quality of the kinds of things [he and The Beatles] did in producing what they produced.

It was a very impressive case."

— Hon. Thomas P. Griesa,
US District Court, Southern District of New York, 1974–2017
Chief Judge, 1993–2000
"Hon. Thomas P. Griesa: An Oral History"

For All Who Admired
John Winston Ono Lennon

"I am [qualified to tell the court how the public was confused by the bootleg *Roots* album]. I met the public, who talked to me about my product. I met a taxi driver who said, 'Sorry, I already bought the wrong one.' That is the public. They talk to me on the street. I know what they are thinking. I don't live in some ivory tower. I walk the streets. I get in taxicabs and I know what they think."

— John Lennon
Trial testimony, April 1, 1976

Contents

FOREWORD

I MET JOHN LENNON SHORTLY AFTER HE ARRIVED IN NEW
YORK IN 1971. We were friends until his untimely death. At
John's invitation I attended some of the *John Lennon Rock 'n'
Roll* album trial, where his testimony fascinated me.

The crux of the case was that John gave Morris Levy
a "rough mix" tape of *Rock 'n' Roll*, which Morris released.
Against John's wishes and the contractual obligations John had
with Capitol/EMI, Morris even produced TV ads to promote
the bootleg album. To prove he hadn't intended for Morris
to release the album, John explained in detail the difference
between "a rough mix," a final mix, and a lacquer master from
which a record is cut. On the witness stand John told the trial
judge exactly, in detail, how he produced an album of songs.

I always thought John's explanations of his artistic and
technical methods should be made available to his world of
fans and anyone interested in the recording process. Jay often
said these gems were part of the trial transcript, but who would
think of looking for them there and who, other than a practic-
ing lawyer, would know how to find them?

Some people are more interesting than others; John Lennon was among the most interesting and charismatic. He's the
kind of client people remember as a career highlight. And so
it is with Jay: he had a long, successful career, but most people
he meets want to know about the case he handled for the most
famous member of the most famous band in the world, The
Beatles.

After years of informal reminiscing, Jay organized his
story into a public talk, which became very successful. He

first delivered it at the Tryon Fine Arts Center in rural North Carolina, moved to the bigger Peace Center for the Performing Arts in Greenville, South Carolina, and then returned the story to New York at the 92nd Street Y, where I saw him present it. Then I really started nudging Jay to write it all down and find a publisher so more people could access John's story. This book is the finished result.

People often ask me what John Lennon was like. I usually tell them the best way to find out is through John's own words. *Lennon, the Mobster & the Lawyer: The Untold Story* reveals the John Lennon I knew as he describes his artistic process and shows his keen sense of humor. This book is much more than a trial transcript, though. Jay tells many stories of his interactions with John and what he was like as a person, capturing how much fun it was to be with John Lennon and Yoko Ono.

Jay has shone a light on an unknown part of John Lennon's life that was not about fame, luxury, or success. He presents John at a time of crisis and problem solving. It's fascinating to learn about John's dedication to solving this problem, how he got into it, and how Jay successfully got him out.

I hope you enjoy learning this untold story as much as I did.

Bob Gruen
New York City
November 2021

Bob Gruen is an internationally renowned photographer who has photographed many of the major artists in rock and roll music.

INTRODUCTION

1996

I TOOK A CLIENT TO LUNCH AT SLOPPY LOUIE'S, near the Lower Manhattan fish market district. The name said it all. A humble yet excellent seafood restaurant, Louie's was located in a dilapidated early 1800s building off the southwest corner of South and Fulton streets. Twenty years had passed since I'd been there with my most interesting client—someone whose friendship had changed my life.

As we waited for a table, I noticed a framed cover of The Beatles' *Red Album* on the wall. John Lennon had autographed it.

"How come The Beatles' album signed by John Lennon?" I asked the cashier.

"Years ago he and Yoko Ono used to come in for lunch every day with a bunch of lawyers," the cashier replied. "They'd always sit at that table over there in the back. Guess the two of them liked the food because later they came in alone. One day we asked John if he'd autograph the album cover. He gladly did."

I turned to the table he pointed out and was suddenly catapulted into the past. I saw myself having lunch with John, Yoko, and my colleague, Howard Roy. We'd just come from the trial where I was representing John against the Mafia-connected record mogul Morris Levy. What lively conversations we'd had before we returned to court. I was back in the '70s again, sitting at a plain dark wood table, enjoying a plate of Louie's famous Long Island Calamari, drinking from a small plastic cup. There was a basket of bread on the table for all of us to share.

How did that happen? How did I, Jay Bergen, wind up representing John Lennon in a major court case? How did we become friends? How did this friendship change me?

Herein lies the story as it unfolded from my front row seat. This book, I think, will be of value to any fan of John Lennon or The Beatles not only for the courtroom drama that unfolded, but also for John Lennon's testimony in which he had to outline for the presiding judge his creative process: for songwriting, for the musicians he handpicked for his recordings, for the recording process in the studio, for the post-production work so few understand is instrumental in the final product listeners hear, and just for the brilliance and interior thoughts from a genius like John Lennon.

It is also valuable to understand John's mindset as he entered a creative hibernation; he didn't record again for almost six years. And after those last recording sessions the world lost one of its great creative musical minds. The world still mourns.

Jay Bergen
Saluda, North Carolina
October 2021

LENNON, the MOBSTER & the LAWYER

THE UNTOLD STORY

Chapter 1

John and Jay Meet

February 3, 1975
Capitol Records
New York City

My partner at our Park Avenue law firm handed me a January 9, 1975 letter from Roulette Records, Inc. It was addressed to him, David Dolgenos, at Marshall, Bratter, Greene, Allison & Tucker and signed by a Morris Levy.

"Can you go to a 5 o'clock meeting at Capitol Records?" David asked. "Their lawyers are discussing a John Lennon bootleg record that this Morris Levy is threatening to release. If there's litigation I want you to handle it."

David had become John Lennon's lawyer in March 1973 during The Beatles' complicated partnership dissolution. I'd heard office rumors about the bootleg album and told David I wanted to be involved.

Excited, I read Levy's letter as I walked back to my office. It claimed that "a stipulation of settlement entered into on October 14 [*sic*], 1973, was breeched [*sic*] by John Lennon." It further said the breach "was resolved during meetings with John Lennon, Harold Sider [*sic*] (John Lennon's attorney), and myself . . . John Lennon has recorded sixteen (16) sides [songs] which I will market throughout the world by use of television advertising."

With several copies of the letter in my attaché, I walked across Fifty-Fifth Street to Capitol's offices on Sixth Avenue.

The Beatles!

By early 1964, I'd bought several of their albums. That July I took my then wife, Betty, to see their first movie, *A Hard Day's Night*.

"These guys are for real!" I told her, as we walked back to our Brooklyn apartment. "That was a very clever funny movie."

Betty and I were among sixteen thousand fans who saw The Beatles live at Forest Hills Stadium in Queens on August 28, 1964. They landed in a helicopter on a back tennis court. The main court was blocked by police sawhorses. Yet a young woman managed to reach the stage, run past John and Paul, and grab George around the waist from behind. It took two security guards to pry her loose. He never stopped playing his guitar or laughing.

I could practically hear that crowd as I entered Capitol's offices. In a room with a conference table and chairs, framed posters and photos of Capitol recording artists on the walls, I met Solomon Granett and Jerrold Gold, partners in Granett & Gold, a law firm that represented Capitol, and Charles Tillinghast, a lawyer from Capitol's Los Angeles headquarters.

"I'm Jay Bergen," I said. "David Dolgenos asked me to come to the meeting because John Lennon and Capitol may get involved in litigation with this Morris Levy." I handed them copies of Levy's January 9 letter. They hadn't seen it.

"We're planning to release a Lennon album called *John Lennon Rock 'n' Roll* in March or April," Tillinghast said. "It contains Lennon's versions of ten rock and roll oldies, including 'Be-Bop-A-Lula,' 'Tutti Frutti,' 'Stand by Me,' and others from that era."

"I know those songs," I said. "They were popular when I was in high school. They're great songs and classic records."

Granett jumped in.

"We learned last Thursday [January 30] that Levy is going to release a record similar to or maybe the same as Capitol's album," he said. "He's calling it *Roots*."

The door opened and in walked John Lennon—a huge surprise to me. His clothes, neat and clean, looked like he'd bought them at a secondhand store or the Salvation Army—tan slacks, a light-colored shirt with a casually tied paisley tie, a brown sport jacket, dark winter coat, black cap, and his trademark wire rim glasses. *He's John Lennon*, I thought. *He can dress however he wants.*

We lawyers were dressed in our uniforms—suits, dress shirts, ties, polished (maybe) shoes. We introduced ourselves and shook hands. *I'm in a meeting with John Lennon*, I thought, *the John Lennon of The Beatles*. I explained why I was there and showed him Levy's letter.

"Have you seen this?" I asked. He scanned it.

"No," he replied.

"Did you agree that you'd record sixteen sides that Levy could sell worldwide using TV advertising?"

"I never made any agreement with him," John said. "I hardly know the man. I don't do business deals. And I didn't make any recordings with or for him."

John explained that Levy had sued in 1970, claiming "Come Together," which John wrote, infringed the copyright on Chuck Berry's "You Can't Catch Me," owned by Big Seven Music, a Levy publishing company. John settled the case by agreeing to record three of Levy's classic rock songs on an oldies record he was working on in October 1973.

Levy had pestered John to hear his three songs. Last November, to get Levy off his back, John had two "rough mix" reel-to-reel tapes of the unfinished album delivered to Levy, so he could listen to his songs in his office. Levy was going to use those tapes to sell *Roots* on TV.

"They're not the final version of my album," John said. "I might have to delete some crummy tracks and it's too long." Visibly upset, he added, "My fans will hate it."

I turned to John with an idea.

"How much time will it take to finish the album?"

"Two days to do some final mixing, decide about cutting two of the tracks, then make the final parts and ship them to Capitol."

"What about that?" I asked Capitol's lawyers. "How soon after that can you release *Rock 'n' Roll?*"

"A week or so," Tillinghast replied. I looked at John.

"I'd rather finish it now," he said. "It's been too long. I'm tired and sick of it. Never had a record take this long. I'll go to Record Plant tomorrow and finish it."

Record Plant Studios was a New York recording studio where John often worked. We had a plan and he was happy with it.

He and I left the meeting and went into the elevator together.

"Are you one of the lawyers?" he asked. *He doesn't remember who I am*, I thought, *but he will as we get to know each other*.

"Yes," I said, "but don't hold that against me." He laughed. As we walked through the lobby, he turned to me.

"You forgot your coat," he said.

"I only wear a scarf," I answered, holding it up. John gave me a quizzical look.

"Well, I'm going home," he said. "Good night."

We walked together into the cold night. As I walked east on Fifty-Fifth Street toward my office at 430 Park Avenue, it hit me. I just advised John Lennon on business/legal strategy. Amazing!

Unbeknownst to me and even more astonishing was the friendship the two of us would develop—John, the thirty-four-year-old rock icon, and Jay, the thirty-seven-year-old, buttoned-down, "just the facts, ma'am" lawyer. I could not have fathomed that night where my representation of John Lennon would take me.

Chapter 2

The Dramatis Personae

February 4, 1975
430 Park Avenue
New York City

THE NEXT MORNING I ASKED MY SECRETARY, Pat Kennedy, "please get me the file on a case called Big Seven Music against Maclen Music from the file room.

"We're going to be representing John Lennon in some possible litigation," I said.

I reported to David about the meeting.

"John endorsed my idea of finishing the album and having Capitol release it as quickly as possible," I said. "He'll be working in the studio today and tomorrow to finish it. Say, who is this Harold Seider referred to in Levy's January 9 letter?"

"He's a lawyer who had worked for Allen Klein when Klein was managing John, George Harrison, and Ringo Starr," David said. "Harold is now a vice president of United Artists Records and Music Group in Los Angeles. He's John's business adviser. When John needed a New York attorney, Harold referred him to me. Seider is in New York now. I'll arrange for you to meet him."

"Who else should I speak to?"

"May Pang," David replied.

"Who's she?" I asked.

"May Pang worked for Klein and then became John and Yoko Ono's full-time assistant. In mid-1973, John and Yoko were having marital problems. Yoko kicked John out of their apartment and pushed him to be with May. She and John were together during his crazy time in Los Angeles, his so-called 'lost weekend,' until near the end of last year."

"If we need her as a witness," I asked, "is she going to be hostile to John over their breakup?"

"She'll probably be okay," David replied.

Finally, I turned my attention to Morris Levy. David said Levy was a crook who cheated recording artists signed to his record companies. Either he didn't pay them record royalties or he put his name on their songs as a cowriter, thereby claiming a portion of their publishing royalties even though he hadn't written a note. Looking for a payoff via a quick settlement, Levy also filed copyright infringement cases.

I later researched Morris Levy's background. The condensed story about him convinced me he was well connected to the Mafia.

On July 13, 1973, Gerald Martin Zelmanowitz, a convicted securities swindler, testified before the Permanent Subcommittee on Investigation of the United States Senate Committee on Government Operations. Zelmanowitz was in the US witness protection program after testifying in a 1970 trial that led to the conviction and imprisonment of Angelo "Gyp" DeCarlo, a member of the New York Genovese crime family in charge of loan sharking operations in New Jersey.

Zelmanowitz testified that DeCarlo had, "in association with Roulette Records, a major recording firm in New York City . . . a so-called piece of [the singing group Frankie Valli and The Four Seasons] and its earnings." He added that DeCarlo had an "interest" in Roulette Records whose "principal is Morris Levy." That "interest" was "[i]n partnership with Thomas Eboli, who is now dead. His name is Tommy Ryan, he was called."

I learned who Thomas Eboli was in a July 17, 1972, *New York Times* article headlined "A Key Gang Figure Slain In Brooklyn." After the 1969 death of Vito Genovese "in a Federal penitentiary, Eboli shared caretaker leadership of the

Genovese crime family with Gerardo 'Jerry' Catena and Michele 'Mike' Miranda, an elder in the underworld." On July 17 Eboli was found at 1 a.m. "sprawled face down on the sidewalk . . . [in the Crown Heights district of Brooklyn]. There were five bullet holes in Eboli's face and neck."

These reports showed that Morris Levy was not simply in the recording and music publishing businesses. Thomas Eboli had been his partner in Roulette Records along with Angelo DeCarlo, maybe silently. Both were high-ranking members of the Mafia. Thomas Eboli had been assassinated gangland style. Levy was not a member of the Mafia because he was Jewish, but he might as well have been.

The real back story was that Levy was a "business" associate of Vincent "The Chin" Gigante, reputed head of the Genovese crime family.

David handed me several record albums as I left his office—Elton John's *Greatest Hits*, Ringo Starr's *Goodnight Vienna*, and John Lennon's *Imagine, Mind Games*, and *Walls and Bridges*. I couldn't wait to get home and listen to them.

Back in my office, the file on Levy's 1970 copyright infringement suit told me that Levy's case was based solely on Chuck Berry's lyric in "You Can't Catch Me," "Here come a flattop," referring to a convertible. But John Lennon's "Come Together" lyric, "Here come old flat top," referenced a man who once had a crew cut.

The lawsuit was just another one of Morris Levy's bogus quick threaten-and-settle scams.

Levy had figured out a way to get his hooks into John Lennon. John would be required to record three of Levy's songs "on his next album," an oldies album that Phil Spector was producing in October 1973.

His songs were rock 'n' roll classics from the '50s and '60s. It seemed to me John had taken an artistic chance doing cover versions of them. Granted, Levy would earn music publishing royalties with three of his songs on John's oldies album. However, even if the album sold one million copies at a royalty of approximately two cents per song per record, that would total only sixty thousand dollars.

By day's end I had greater insight into the brewing dispute between John/Capitol Records and Morris Levy. If the dispute flared into litigation, it would be fascinating to represent John.

I gathered up my new record albums and left for home. I'd lost touch with rock and roll when I moved with Betty and our daughter to St. Croix in the Virgin Islands in June 1966. After three years at a Wall Street law firm, I had resigned and joined a small firm in Christiansted, St. Croix, that paid me more than I'd earned in New York.

I found out quickly I should have stayed in New York. After months of suspicions and some clever detective work on my own, I discovered my wife was having an affair with another lawyer in the firm. Even though my evidence of the affair was rock solid, I didn't confront her. I'd been programmed early in life not to question, not to confront, to just follow instructions. Though I was twenty-nine years old, I had no voice. We muddled through the days. Time passed painfully. Finally, we separated and she filed for divorce. In December 1967 I returned to New York alone and rejoined the law firm I'd left eighteen months earlier.

As a litigator I was calm, focused, and decisive, but my personal life was sometimes chaotic and impulsive. While separated from Betty, I met a woman who'd been born in St. Croix. We married in July 1968, shortly after Betty and I divorced.

Rock and roll wasn't popular in our house since she loved Caribbean music. So when I returned to New York, I didn't get back into the music, which once had been a huge part of my life. I'd fallen in love with rock and roll in high school when I heard songs like the Penguins' "Earth Angel" on the radio. I'd gone to New York disc jockey Alan Freed's rock and roll shows at the Brooklyn and Times Square Paramount theaters. In college I'd seen Elvis Presley live in Philadelphia in 1957.

When I got home that night, I was reintroduced to so much I'd missed. I played side one of Elton John's album. I played some tracks from *Goodnight Vienna* and the moving title track from *Imagine*. Not only was I John Lennon's lawyer, but I was back where I belonged—listening to rock and roll. I was home.

Chapter 3

Just the Facts

February 6, 1975
Capitol Records
New York City

I MET CAPITOL'S LAWYERS IN THE SAME CONFERENCE ROOM WE'D USED THREE DAYS EARLIER. This time John Lennon, May Pang, and Harold Seider joined us. Capitol had learned that Morris Levy was buying airtime on TV stations for *Roots* commercials. Capitol would release *Rock 'n' Roll* the following week. I needed to learn more about the facts.

"I have good news, mates!" John announced. "I finished the album and the metal parts are being shipped to Capitol today for pressing and release." He was happy and looked relieved.

"That's great, John," Harold said. "You cut 'Angel Baby' and 'Be My Baby,' right?"

"Yes, they were too long and a mess," John replied.

Harold provided some basic facts. He talked about *Walls and Bridges,* an album of John's original songs except for a brief version of "Ya Ya," the last track that features John singing and his son, Julian, playing drums.

"After *Walls and Bridges* came out in mid-September," Harold said, "Morris called me, complaining, 'Where are my three songs? *Walls and Bridges* is John's next album but it has only one of my songs on it, "Ya Ya." Where are my other two songs?' I explained how Phil Spector had disappeared with the master tapes of the oldies album in December 1973, but he wouldn't listen."

"He kept claiming this was John's 'next' album," Harold continued. "Morris knew *Walls and Bridges* was an album of John's songs. He kept saying that John's 'next' album, according to the October 1973 settlement, was supposed to be the oldies album. Finally, Morris demanded: 'I want to hear the story from John Lennon himself.'"

In other words, Morris Levy wanted to meet John Lennon. That was the beginning of Morris's scam.

Harold arranged for John and Morris to meet on October 8, 1974 at the Club Cavallero, a New York restaurant/bar where Levy was a member. They were a party of six—Harold; John; May Pang; Bernard Brown, an employee of The Beatles company, Apple Corps Limited, in England; Morris; and Phil Kahl, a Big Seven employee.

"Harold said it would be a good thing if I met Morris," John explained. "I was nervous about meeting him. I didn't know him and Harold told me he was annoyed with me. I explained to Morris that Spector had been taking home the master tapes of each session. Then he didn't show up at the studio one night last December. He had the tapes. He disappeared. Recording stopped. I couldn't contact Phil. Neither could Capitol. Phil is very strange. You never know what's going to happen with him."

While he was waiting for the master tapes to be found, John produced *Pussy Cats*, a Harry Nilsson album, in Los Angeles. He wrote new songs, too. In July, when he was about to begin recording those new songs, Capitol retrieved the master tapes from Spector and shipped twenty-eight boxes of them to John at Record Plant.

"I told Morris I had reviewed a few boxes and realized many tapes were in poor condition," John said. "I told him I knew I'd need to spend a lot of time listening to them and, though some tracks might be salvageable, I'd have to re-record others. So I decided to go ahead with the scheduled recordings of my new songs, as I'd planned. Those recordings became *Walls and Bridges*."

The factual picture became clearer in my mind.

"I told Morris I was worried about releasing the oldies album even when it was completed," John told me.

"Why?" I asked.

"It had been almost a year since we began recording in LA. There'd been a lot of negative publicity about the recording sessions," John said. "I called it my 'lost weekend.' Lots of drinking and carousing.

"I was worried the critics were waiting to criticize the album. I'd even thought about selling the album on TV. That way I could sell it directly to my fans and avoid the critics. I told Morris all this."

At the mention of TV marketing, Levy had perked up.

"He said he had a company that advertised and sold records on TV," Harold explained. "He said, 'I can sell the album!'"

Harold and John immediately told Levy that John had an exclusive contract with EMI Records—and that EMI had to grant permission to sell the album on TV.

"Everyone in the music industry, including Morris, knows that John and the other Beatles have been signed to exclusive agreements with EMI since the early '60s," Harold said. "We didn't have to tell Morris that. But he asked, 'When are you going to England to get EMI's permission?' I told him such a request was premature."

At that point John had invited Morris to come to Record Plant the next morning to hear some of the tracks. *Another meeting!*

That revelation led to more: John had met Levy several times over the remainder of 1974.

John and May occasionally had gone to the Club Cavallero. One night John mentioned his musicians were coming to New York to rehearse the oldies songs and record them at Record Plant. When Levy heard this, he invited John and the band to his Sunnyview Farm upstate in Ghent, New York.

"He said we could rehearse there," John said. "I said no.

He kept asking. I declined several times."

May Pang interjected.

"I left the table," she recalled. "When I returned John told me, 'We're going to Morris's farm.' I said, 'You told Morris no several times. What happened?' John replied, 'I ran out of excuses.'"

Apparently, John had a problem saying "no" to people sometimes. He said it would have been rude to tell Levy he just didn't want to go.

And so on the weekend of October 18–20, 1974, John went to the farm with the band—Jesse Ed Davis (lead guitar), Klaus Voormann (bass), Jim Keltner (drums), Kenny Ascher (keyboards), and Eddie Mottau (acoustic guitar).

"How many times did you and Levy get together at the Club Cavallero?" I asked John.

"I don't know, but Morris kept pestering me. He wanted to listen to his three songs," John said. "Finally, one night in November when we were at the club, I asked him, 'What do you want—a cassette or a tape?' Morris said, 'A reel-to-reel tape so I can play it in my office.' I called Record Plant and told them to make two reel-to-reel tapes of the album and bring them to the Club. I gave them to Morris. At that point they were an unfinished 'rough mix.' I thought that would get him off my back. He must be using those tapes to manufacture this *Roots* album."

Yes, I thought, *he certainly must be.*

"When John told me about Morris having the tapes," Harold said, "I told him I wished he hadn't done that."

Levy finally had set the trap. John put his foot in, and it snapped shut.

"What about Levy's January 9 letter?" I asked Harold. "Was it ever answered?"

In a word, no. When David Dolgenos had received the letter, he'd phoned Harold about it and mailed it to him. Harold said he'd take care of it. Instead Harold and Levy had argued on the phone.

"Morris called me in January," Harold said. "He asked me again about getting EMI's permission. I told him I hadn't done that yet. He yelled at me, 'Then I'm going to send a letter saying John and I have a deal.' I said, 'Morris, we don't have a deal, but I'm not going to get into a shit kicking contest with you.' He hung up on me.

"I had lunch with Al Coury, Capitol's VP of A&R [artist and repertoire] at the Brown Derby in LA on January 9," Harold added. "I told Coury about the situation with Morris. He didn't like the idea of selling the oldies album on TV. He wanted to hear the album. I arranged for May to send Al a cassette of the album.

"I called Morris the following Monday. I told him about my meeting with Coury and his request to hear the album. Morris said, 'Oh, oh, that is bad.' (I thought, *Levy knew Capitol would want to release* Rock 'n' Roll *and would not agree to sell it via TV advertising.*)

"When Capitol heard the album, they got excited about it," Harold explained. "They wanted to set up a meeting with John in New York to go over a marketing plan. I didn't answer Morris's letter. I'd told him several times that we didn't have a deal."

That was definitely not good. I turned to John.

"Did you have a meeting with Capitol about the album?" I asked.

"Yes," he answered. "Harold, May, and I met with Al Coury and Capitol's marketing people. I told them about my TV idea and how it would avoid the critics. They didn't like the idea. They explained that the album should be marketed the way all Beatles and John Lennon albums had been sold. They were concerned that cutting out mom-and-pop record stores and big retail chains would cause an uproar in the industry. They said there'd be a lot of bad press aimed at me and Capitol."

The Capitol marketers laid out a plan with ads and other suggestions. After a while, John said, he realized they were right: a TV sale would be a mistake.

"I told them I had an idea for a cover photo," John said. "I knew a photographer in Hamburg, Jürgen Vollmer, who had taken photos of me and the other Beatles. There was a black-and-white shot of me standing in a doorway that I really liked. I knew Jürgen was living in Brooklyn. They were able to call him right then and make a deal for the photo. We decided on the name, *Rock 'n' Roll*, and that was it."

The next day, January 29, Harold called Levy and told him that Capitol wanted to market the album. He also said EMI would not give permission for a TV sale. Levy was not happy. He asked Harold to come to his office the next day.

"When I arrived," Harold said, "Morris was sitting at his desk. His lawyer, Bill Krasilovsky, arrived a few minutes later. I didn't like the looks of it. When I started to explain about Capitol's decision and how John had no choice, Morris turned around and pushed a button on a reel-to-reel tape recorder behind him. I was now listening to John Lennon singing 'You Can't Catch Me,' obviously from the tapes John had given to Morris."

"Krasilovsky is the attorney who filed the 'Come Together' copyright infringement case for Levy, correct?" I said.

"Yes," replied Harold. "Morris started cursing and yelling at me, 'I'm going to put it out! I've got a shot! I've got a shot!' I told Morris that Capitol would get an injunction. In the middle of all this, the door opened and I was introduced to William Schurtman, another lawyer."

"Who's William Schurtman?" I asked.

"I don't know," Harold said. "He was introduced by Morris as his lawyer. I didn't ask any questions. I knew then we were looking at litigation and kept quiet. 'Do you want to call Capitol?' Morris asked me. I stared out the window. There was a three-way conversation among Morris and his two lawyers. I was in the middle of a Morris pressure tactic. I had to get out of there. I got up and left. That was last Thursday."

"Any other contacts with Levy, John?" I asked.

"Yes," John explained. "I mentioned to him one night at the club that my son, Julian, was coming for Christmas. Morris invited us to go to Disney World with him and his son because his son was almost the same age as Julian. So in December, May, Julian, and I flew to Orlando and stayed at a condo of a friend of Morris's for a few days."

A family trip to Florida!

"When you and Levy were together in Florida, did you talk any more about his wanting to market the oldies album on TV?" I asked.

"No," John replied. "From the first meeting at the Club Cavallero I made it clear to Morris any time he mentioned a deal that I didn't talk business. Business isn't my thing. It's not my job. He finally stopped trying to get me to talk about it."

All of John's contact with Levy over an almost three-month period got me thinking. *This is going to be a problem if there is litigation. It's not going to look good if John Lennon and Morris Levy are "hanging out" after the meeting at the Club Cavallero. Also, there was no written response to Levy's January 9 letter. It's going to look like there was some kind of agreement between them.*

Both John and Harold assured the Capitol attorneys several times that John did not make any agreement with Levy. In fact, John said he told Levy, "It's cool with me to sell the album on TV as long as it's alright with the record company. I'm exclusively with EMI. EMI owns everything I do, even if I speak."

After a couple of hours, the meeting ended and I went downstairs with John, Harold, and May.

"I think the meeting went well," I said in the lobby. "We'll just have to wait for Levy's next move. He's going to release some version of the oldies album and the Capitol album will be released soon."

John was amazed Levy would do such a thing but knew then it was a real possibility. We said goodbye.

Deep in thought, I walked back to my office. *It doesn't make any sense that John Lennon would make an agreement with Morris Levy at that meeting. He'd never met Levy before.*

First, that wasn't the purpose of the meeting. John was there to tell Levy that Phil Spector had caused the interruption of the oldies recording sessions and that he was going to resume working on the album.

Second, according to John, Harold, and May Pang, there wasn't any discussion of the terms and conditions of an agreement, such as the payment of recording costs or royalties or any of the many provisions that needed to be negotiated.

Third, nothing was reduced to writing and signed by the parties then or at a later date. In fact, there wasn't even any discussion of a written agreement.

Finally, John had made it clear he wasn't free to make any agreement with Levy with respect to the oldies album. John and Harold had told Levy that EMI's permission was necessary. Levy already knew that.

Of course, I knew it wasn't going to be that simple. Morris Levy was a grifter and his grift was underway.

Chapter 4

Levy and His Two Lawsuits

February 7, 1975
New York City

THE DAY AFTER OUR MEETING, Capitol and John sent telegrams to TV stations to warn them about *Roots*. The message was urgent: "EMI OWNS THE MASTERS OF THE JOHN LENNON ALBUM ABOUT TO BE OR BEING ADVERTISED ON YOUR STATION, WHICH IS AN UNAUTHORIZED RELEASE."

The following Tuesday, John called me. Jimmy Iovine, a Record Plant engineer who had worked with John and Phil Spector on the LA recording sessions, had called John on Saturday, February 8. He'd just seen a TV ad for *John Lennon Sings The Great Rock & Roll Hits – Roots*.

"Jimmy asked me what was going on. I said, 'Bloody hell if I know,'" John said. "I spent all day Saturday and Sunday watching TV, trying to see it. I saw it once but it was too quick to get any details."

On February 13, Capitol shipped 342,000 copies of *John Lennon Rock 'n' Roll*.

Levy stopped the *Roots* TV advertising on February 17. Two days later, Big Seven and Adam VIII, Levy's TV marketing company, sued John, Apple Records, Harold, Capitol, and EMI in New York Supreme Court. Their lawyers were Walter, Conston, Schurtman & Gumpel, P.C. The Schurtman was the William Schurtman who had joined the January 30 Seider trap in Levy's office.

The complaint's "First Cause Of Action" alleged that "Apple and Lennon have breached the October 1974 Agreement," claiming damages "in the sum of $7,000,000," an outlandish amount. The premise of the complaint was the so-called "agreement" reached between Levy and John at the October 8, 1974 Club Cavallero meeting. There was no claim of a written agreement. It also alleged six other causes of action.

Schurtman should have known better than to allege extremely high damages. He used a timeworn but transparent tactic designed to strike fear in defendants. I didn't think Big Seven and Adam VIII could possibly prove anything close to $7 million! Additionally, $15 million alleged in punitive damages claims, rarely awarded under New York law, was ridiculous. I called John.

"Morris Levy has started a lawsuit against you, Harold, Apple, Capitol, and EMI, based on the October 8 meeting," I said. "They're claiming that you made an agreement that night to sell the oldies album on TV using Levy's company. Unsurprisingly, there's no allegation that there's anything in writing to evidence such an agreement."

"But I never made any agreement that night with Morris," John said. "Harold and I told Morris I was signed to EMI. We said that if the oldies album was going to be sold on TV, EMI would have to agree to do that."

"I know, John. These are just claims made in a complaint," I said. "I don't believe that Levy is going to be able to prove them. Look, the damage claims are outlandish. Don't worry about the $7 million and $15 million amounts. They're bogus, fake, supposed to scare you."

"Jay, this is bad. I'm really worried that I'll have to pay Morris Levy a lot of money. I just want to hold down the amount I'll have to pay Morris," he said. "This is very important."

"John, I'm going to do everything I can to make sure you won't have to pay Levy anything," I replied. "The fact they've alleged meaningless damages tells me that Levy gave them grossly inflated numbers to scare you. I'll have a copy of the complaint delivered to you tomorrow. If you have any questions, call me."

I read him one allegation in the complaint I wanted to check: ". . . in or about November 1974, Lennon, working together with representatives of Big Seven, recorded the album and delivered to Big Seven two master tapes containing the 15 selections."

"Did you work with Big Seven people or anybody who worked for Levy?" I asked.

"Of course not," John said. "I never worked with anyone connected to Morris. He's talking about the 'rough mix' tapes I told you about. All the work was done at Record Plant. No one from Big Seven was involved. Jay, call Jimmy Iovine at Record Plant. He'll be able to tell you what was given to Morris."

He gave me Record Plant's telephone number. The next day, I called and introduced myself to Jimmy Iovine.

"I'm representing John Lennon in a lawsuit filed by Morris Levy over the oldies album. He asked me to call you," I said. "What do you know about two reel-to-reel tapes of the oldies album that were given to Morris Levy last November?"

"I made those tape copies of sides one and two of the oldies album," Jimmy replied.

"Were they master tapes? That's what Levy claims John had given him."

"They were not master tapes," he said. "They were two 7-1/2 ips half-track EQ tapes."

"What does ips mean?" I asked.

"Inches per second, meaning how fast the tape is turning in the tape machine," he explained. "This type of tape is good quality but not good enough so that John would release it as an album. It is a fairly good representation of the album, but the album wasn't finished at that point. It was a 'rough mix.'"

Later I learned that in 1974/75 the industry standard for master tapes was 15 ips. They were used to manufacture the best quality records, although some recording artists were beginning to use 30 ips tapes.

Twelve days later, John sent me a copy of the New York summons and complaint, along with his handwritten note:

"4 March 1975 Received this today from Ms. Bockin of the Dakota office. She said someone arrived at 1W72 around 7 AM and when the doorman wouldn't let him in, the person taped the document to a part of the building. John"

On March 6, much to my surprise, Levy's lawyers filed another complaint against the same defendants, in federal court. As required by federal rules, it was signed by William Schurtman, "A Member of the Firm."

The federal complaint repeated the false allegations about an October 1974 agreement between John and Levy and that ". . . in or about 1974, Lennon, working together with representatives of Big Seven, recorded the album and delivered to Big Seven two master tapes containing the 15 selections."

This complaint alleged a violation of Sections 1 and 2 of the Sherman Antitrust Act in that the defendants "conspired with one another to prevent plaintiffs from promoting and selling the album successfully in interstate and foreign commerce and to monopolize the trade for recordings by Lennon." It alleged that "Plaintiffs have been damaged in the sum of $14 million." The so-called Sherman Act provides that any damage award is automatically trebled, meaning that Levy's (and Schurtman's) real damages claim, if proved, was $42 million! It was laughable.

I called John. He was alarmed.

"What does this mean? Why has he filed another case?"

"Levy's trying to put pressure on you," I said. "He wants you to come to him to reach a settlement. I don't know who dreamed this one up, but it was a big mistake by Levy and Schurtman. The case has been assigned 'for all purposes' to Judge Lloyd MacMahon. That means he'll be the judge in charge of all aspects of the case, including the trial.

"John, I know Judge MacMahon. He knows my firm and one of my partners. He's been a federal judge for seventeen years. He does not put up with any nonsense from lawyers. He runs a very fast calendar, too. He will push us and Levy's lawyers to move the case quickly to a trial. This is good news for us and bad news for Levy."

"You sound confident. I don't want to settle with Morris, Jay. I want to be rid of him," John said. "I'm tired of these phony legal cases. I want to put a stop to them. The United States wants to deport me and Allen Klein's filed a ridiculous case. I don't want to do any deals with Morris. He wants to cheat me like he's cheated other singers and songwriters. I've heard about him."

"I understand," I said. "This is the time to make a stand. We have an advantage. I think the $14 million damage claim is more outlandish than the state court damages claims. State court cases move very slowly, take forever to get to trial. We should push this federal case as hard as we can to a trial.

"I'll send you a copy of the complaint. If you have any questions, call me."

John sounded determined: he wouldn't be bullied by this second lawsuit. *It's not going to work,* I thought. *John and I are developing a good relationship. He's gaining confidence in my advice.*

Chapter 5

The Yoko Audition

The Dakota. BOB GRUEN

March 1975
The Dakota
New York City

A FEW DAYS LATER, JOHN CALLED. He asked me to meet Yoko at their apartment at 11 o'clock the next morning.

"Sure," I said. "Should I bring anything with me?"

"No, Yoko would like to meet you."

John and Yoko Ono had moved to the Dakota in 1973. They bought a seventh-floor apartment from actor Robert

Ryan's estate. Ryan had appeared in ninety-one movies and TV shows between 1940 and 1973, including Sam Peckinpah's classic Western, *The Wild Bunch*.

The Dakota, a famous luxury apartment house, is on the northwest corner of Seventy-Second Street and Central Park West. Built in the early 1880s when that area of Manhattan Island, far north and west, was virtually uninhabited, it was named after the Dakota Territory. The building was designated a New York City landmark in 1969 and a US National Historic Landmark seven years later.

The apartments are large—nine rooms is not unusual—with wood-paneled walls and inlaid floors of mahogany, oak, and cherry. Some drawing rooms are forty-nine feet long with fourteen-foot ceilings. Above the archway entrance on Seventy-Second Street is the face of a Dakota Indian.

The Dakota doorman showed me to the elevator. As the elevator door opened on the seventh floor and I stepped out, a young man held the door to John and Yoko's apartment open. I stepped into a large drawing room with windows to the east, overlooking Central Park, and to the south, overlooking Seventy-Second Street. The room was sparsely furnished. John's white Steinway grand piano sat on the south side of the room near a window.

Yoko Ono walked into the room toward me.

"Good morning, Jay," she said. "Thank you for coming."

"Good morning, Yoko." We shook hands. "Nice to meet you. What a great view of Central Park," I said, pointing toward a window.

"Yes, it is a beautiful view, lots of light," she replied. "Please sit down. I wanted to meet you because John and I are very worried about these cases Morris Levy has begun. We want to hold down the amount of money John would have to pay Morris if he loses. John does not want to make any settlement with Morris."

"I understand," I said. "I'll be glad to answer any questions you might have."

She was petite with long black hair flowing loosely below her shoulders. Her large dark eyes were very expressive. Yoko wore a floor-length, loose-fitting black gown. She took a seat on the couch. I took a chair opposite her on the other side of a coffee table. The man who had opened the apartment door placed a tray on the table. It held a small cup and spoon and a cup and saucer. Yoko began eating what looked like black caviar from the small cup. Occasionally she sipped black coffee from the other cup.

Yoko was friendly but businesslike. She asked me a few questions: How long had I been at Marshall Bratter? What was my litigation experience? Did I know anything about Morris Levy?

As she delved into the specifics of Levy's claims, her questions became sharper. She had read both complaints. Her questions told me she was very bright. In her own way she was politely "grilling" me. I was fine with that and glad she was interested. I knew from articles I'd read that she and John were extremely close.

Not until years later did I realize that Yoko Ono was auditioning me that day. She wanted to figure out whether she liked me and believed I was capable of being John's advocate in the courtroom. Yoko wanted to be very sure I was the right lawyer to protect her husband's interests. That was her paramount concern. Had I not passed the "audition," I would have been replaced.

She also wanted me to know she intended to be involved.

I wasn't cowed by her questions. I tried to make sure my answers made her feel confident. I was awed to be representing John Lennon. His interactions with Levy posed complicated factual issues. It would not be an easy case, not that I'd ever been involved in a case one would classify as a "slam dunk." But in the end, Morris Levy and his lawyers were no different from other adversaries I'd faced.

Not being a deeply introspective person, I viewed *Big Seven v. John Lennon* as just another case. At the time I had two other cases I was responsible for, both of which would result in a trial and verdict within the next eighteen months.

But John Lennon was not just another client. It was obvious from talking to John, and now Yoko, that this case was very important to them. I knew nothing short of fully mastering a case would ever satisfy me. This would be particularly true with Judge MacMahon presiding at trial, but I also felt a personal obligation to do my best for John and Yoko.

"Why do you think Morris Levy filed this second case?" Yoko asked.

"I've never had that happen in my career," I replied. "Filing two cases, back to back, against the same parties makes no sense to me. It's puzzling because I believe the antitrust claim is going to be almost impossible to prove. He's alleging that there was a conspiracy among the defendants to prevent him from marketing *Roots*. It's nonsensical. And the $14 million damage claim is crazy.

"In my experience," I added, "lawyers sometimes make high-dollar damages claims I find suspect. I immediately begin thinking that they can't be serious. Damages are very difficult to prove. You have to have real factual bases for proving damages. It's hard. They can't be speculative."

"Why do you say that?" Yoko asked.

"Levy would have to prove that he would have sold millions of copies of his *Roots* album and made an enormous profit per record when he was selling it for only $4.98," I said. "How's he going to be able to do that? I think it's impossible."

"Why is he doing this then?" she asked.

"Because John settled the 'Come Together' case, Levy thinks he'll settle this one. He also has Capitol and EMI as defendants. He may think he'll have an angle to make a deal with them and John. Maybe they'd license records to him that he could market on TV. Levy's a crook, a grifter. He cheats his recording and music publishing artists out of their royalties. He told Harold, 'I'm going to put it out. I've got a shot. I've got a shot.' He's rolling the dice with John and Capitol/EMI.

"I told John filing the federal case was a mistake. It was assigned to a judge who runs a very fast calendar. He's going to move the case to a conclusion quickly. That's great for us. The state court case will plod along at a snail's pace."

Yoko stood up.

"John and I are very worried about these cases," she repeated. "If we have to pay any damages, we want to keep them as low as possible. John does not want to settle with Levy."

"I know. John has been clear that he's not going to give in to Levy's threats. I can't guarantee a result but that's the way to handle this. We have to make Levy prove his case. Working together, John and I can make that very difficult."

"I feel better having spoken to you," Yoko said. She thanked me for coming.

"You're welcome. Anytime you or John have any questions, please call me."

That was a good meeting, I thought as I walked back to the office. *Yoko asked good questions. I answered them satisfactorily.*

The cases were interesting although, as in any case, I had questions. Why did John spend so much time hanging out with Levy? He went to his farm. He accepted invitations to Club Cavallero. He traveled to Florida with Julian and May. Yet Harold had told Levy multiple times that EMI's permission was necessary. John had refused to discuss the TV sale idea with Levy. There was enough to persuade a judge that the case should go to a jury.

As in any case, there would be good facts and bad facts for our side. My job was to emphasize our good facts and play down or nullify any bad ones. I could count on John's availability and he was determined to make Levy prove his case.

Chapter 6

A Walk in the Park (Not on the Wild Side)

April 1975
Central Park
New York City

MARSHALL BRATTER WOULD BE REPRESENTING JOHN AND HAROLD SEIDER (WITH JOHN'S CONSENT). Capitol/EMI were represented by Barrett Prettyman of Hogan & Hartson, a Washington, DC, firm and Sol Granett of Granett & Gold, as New York counsel. Apple was represented by George Grumbach of Cleary, Gottlieb, Steen & Hamilton, a New York firm. As the pre-trial proceedings (witness depositions, production of documents, etc.) got underway, we, the defendants' attorneys, were dealing with Alan Kanzer, a young partner, and Bernard Diamond, a young associate, of William Schurtman's firm. Schurtman was nowhere to be seen.

In order to avoid duplication, it was agreed at the outset that all of the pre-trial depositions, document production, etc., could be used in either the New York State or federal court cases.

While I worked on the Morris Levy cases, David kept track of a case Allen Klein began against John, George Harrison, and Ringo Starr. They were being represented by Cleary Gottlieb. He asked me to observe one day as Klein's lawyers deposed John in that case.

At the end of the day John and I left together and walked uptown on Fifth Avenue. John told me how Klein had become their manager. Paul McCartney didn't like Klein. He preferred to be represented by Lee Eastman and his son John Eastman, brother of Linda Eastman, McCartney's then-girlfriend and later wife. John, George, and Ringo did not like Lee Eastman. They preferred Allen Klein.

"I don't know Lee Eastman but I've had dealings with John Eastman," I said. "I represented Terry Knight, Grand Funk Railroad's founder and manager, in litigation with the members of Grand Funk. John Eastman represented the band. He retained a small copyright and entertainment litigation firm, though, to handle the case between the band and Terry Knight. It involved the usual charges and countercharges between a band and its former manager."

"What did you think of John Eastman?" John asked.

"He was quite impressed with himself," I said. "Thought he was the cat's meow, as they say, but he wasn't. I thought he was a real tight-ass." John laughed, turned to me, and used his rapier-like wit.

"John Eastman was born forty years old, dressed in a dark suit, a white shirt, and a tie."

"That's good! Yes, I know what you mean," I blurted out, laughing. "He was a little on the stiff side."

"If nothing else," John replied, "he certainly was stiff." By then we were both laughing loudly.

"I got involved right after I joined Marshall Bratter in late 1972," I said. "The case had begun earlier in the year. We litigated through 1973. I tried to get settlement talks started several times. A federal magistrate had been appointed to supervise the pre-trial discovery and explore settlement possibilities. At a conference with him to finalize a discovery schedule and discuss settlement, John Eastman appeared with John Clark, the partner in the litigation firm.

"Eastman lost his temper about something I said. He slammed his open palm on the table and yelled at me. It sounded like a gunshot. We all jumped, including the magistrate. He lit into Eastman, asking him, 'What's wrong with you? There's no need for such an outburst.'

"The magistrate's attitude changed dramatically. He began scheduling dates to conclude all depositions and document production and for pre-trial memo filings. He set a possible trial date. The magistrate then raised the question of settlement and scheduled a time later in the week to meet with him to discuss it. To make a long story short, John Eastman blew it. We reached a settlement in early 1974 favorable to Terry Knight."

"That's a great story," John said. "It doesn't surprise me that John Eastman would act out as you described."

We were next to the fountain across from the Plaza Hotel when John suddenly stopped and turned around.

"Just a minute," he said. He walked back to a group of six or seven people standing fifteen feet behind us. I followed him. Nearing them, he politely asked: "You've been following me. What do you want?"

"May we have your autograph?" one asked.

"I'll give you each an autograph," John said, "but then you'll agree to stop following me, okay?"

"Yes. We won't follow you," a couple of them said. "Thank you." Standing on Fifth Avenue, John gave each an autograph.

"Thank you," he said to the group. Then he turned around and we continued toward the entrance to Central Park, crossing Fifty-Ninth Street and going into the park. As we walked toward the West Side, he said he and Yoko were very excited that she was pregnant. I'd been listening to his *Walls and Bridges* album. The songs, written when he and Yoko were separated, told me he'd gone through a rough time.

"Yoko had a miscarriage in 1969," John said. "I want to make sure she doesn't have another one. Her doctor has prescribed bed rest. Do you have any children, Jay?"

"I do," I answered. "I have a ten-year old daughter, by my first marriage, who lives in Tucson, Arizona, and two young girls by my second marriage."

"My son Julian was just twelve," he said.

"Melissa will be eleven in July," I added. "They're only a

year or so apart."

"Do you see your daughter often?" John asked.

"Usually twice a year, alternating Christmas and Easter, and during the summer," I said. "But I don't have any input with respect to her day-to-day upbringing. It's frustrating. I talk to her on the phone. If I go to California on business, I might be able to stop in Tucson on the way home, but that's about it."

"Julian was born in 1963, just as The Beatles thing was starting," John added. "We lost control of it. I was out of touch with Julian when I was around and when I wasn't around. You have no input into your daughter's life. I had no control over me own life for years. I was not a real father to Julian. I don't want that to happen to the child Yoko's carrying. I've been running since we began playing in Hamburg in 1960. Now it's 1975. It's been crazy.

"In the summer of 1973 I began producing my own album," he continued. "I'd never done that before. That was *Mind Games*. Yoko and I separated. May Pang and I went to Los Angeles. I was doing promotion for *Mind Games*.

"I had an idea to do an oldies album, early rock and roll songs from the '50s and '60s. I hired Phil Spector to produce. The recording sessions were a wild scene. I was a scene. One night Phil fired his gun in the bathroom. Phil disappeared with the master tapes.

"Then I helped Harry Nilsson keep his recording contract and produced his album, *Pussy Cats*, last year. Later I started writing some new songs. I was bored."

We were almost to the West Side but John wasn't finished.

"I decided to bring in some of the musicians who had played with us in LA to Record Plant and record the new songs I'd written," he said. "I'd given up on getting the tapes from Phil. Just as May had made all the arrangements at Record Plant and the musicians arrived, those twenty-eight boxes of master tapes arrived from Capitol Records. They'd finally retrieved them from Phil.

"I began listening to the tapes. They were a mess. Twenty-eight musicians playing at the same time. I'm singing in a different key than the musicians on some tracks. I decided to put the tapes aside and record the new songs. I finished *Walls and Bridges*. I worked on the album cover.

"At that point I've still got the oldies tapes waiting for me. You know what happened after that. I'd never spent so much time on an album and it was not finished, not close to being finished. I was exhausted. I wanted to be home. I wanted to be with Yoko. I wasn't. But I had to continue with it until I finished it."

We were standing across from the Dakota.

"I'm sure this won't give you peace of mind," I said, "but that's behind you now. It sounds like quite a run. Thanks for talking about it. It gives me a very good idea of where your head was at when you turned back to the oldies tapes last fall. Then suddenly you're introduced to Morris Levy. This background is important—what your feelings were, what you knew, and when you knew it. Levy's a crook, a bad guy. He's one of those people whose life philosophy is, why do it honestly when I can do it dishonestly?"

"How was this helpful?" John asked.

"Because I'm all about the details in a case," I said. "I want to know more about the facts than my adversary. It's a tremendous advantage to have all the facts, good and bad, down cold. That's why you and I need to have everything out on the table. That way I—and we—can deal with anything that comes up. No surprises."

"Sounds good," John said. "Have a good night."

"You, too." I headed back to the office.

Chapter 7

The Elvis Bond

New York City
April 1975
Central Park

I DRAFTED JOHN'S FORMAL ANSWERS TO THE BIG SEVEN AND
ADAM VIII COMPLAINTS IN THE TWO CASES. In April John
and I discussed them in my office. He needed to understand
the legal and factual positions we were asserting on his behalf. I
knew he'd be questioned about them at his deposition.

We also discussed the two counterclaims John was going to
allege. The first one, against Big Seven and Adam VIII, sought
damages and an injunction for violations of Sections 50 and
51 of the New York Civil Rights Law. Big Seven and Adam
VIII had unlawfully used John Lennon's "picture and likeness
. . . together with his name in connection with the advertise-
ment and sale of . . . *John Lennon Sings The Great Rock & Roll
Hits - Roots*" without his "written or oral consent" and without
"compensation to" him.

The relief requested, in addition to damages suffered by
John because of the unauthorized release of *Roots*, was an injunction prohibiting Big Seven and Adam VIII from selling or
advertising the album in the future.

The second counterclaim, against Big Seven, Adam VIII,
and Morris Levy, also sought damages to John's reputation
resulting from the unauthorized release of *Roots*, an injunction similar to the one sought by the first counterclaim, and an
accounting for any profits these three counterclaim defendants

realized by the illegal *Roots* release.

When John was ready to leave, I said I'd walk with him. I had some additional questions for him.

"Tell me about the idea you had to do this oldies album," I said as we walked west across Fifty-Sixth Street. "Why an album covering early rock 'n' roll hits from the '50s and '60s?"

"I wanted to record, to sing someone else's songs instead of mine or The Beatles'," he said. "I grew up listening to American rock 'n' roll songs. These were the records that I listened to as a teenager that excited me, like 'Angel Baby' by Rosie and the Originals. That's always been one of my all-time favorite records."

"Did you and Phil Spector pick the songs?" I asked. "How did that happen?"

"I had reasons for picking the songs. 'Be Bop-A-Lula' by Gene Vincent was a song my skiffle band, the Quarrymen, played the first time I met Paul, Paul McCartney. We were playing at a church garden fete in Liverpool."

"How old were you?" I asked.

"I was sixteen. I think Paul was fifteen." After we entered Central Park, a teenage boy walked toward us heading in the opposite direction. He recognized John. As the boy walked by John kept talking.

"Another song I liked was 'Bony Moronie' by Larry Williams," John said. "I really liked Larry Williams. I sang that song the only time my mother saw me perform. That's the reason I wanted to sing it. There are others that I had specific reasons for wanting to sing. I'm the only one who knows these reasons. Like 'Ain't That A Shame.' My mother taught me to play that on the banjo."

"Antoine Domino, the Fat Man from New Orleans," I said. "I saw him at an Alan Freed show. I think it was at the Brooklyn Paramount.

"Freed was a popular disc jockey who came to New York from Cleveland in 1954. He was a big hit in New York. That's when I began listening to his show every weekday night on

WINS. He had been playing rhythm and blues records for years in the Midwest. He claimed he was the DJ who coined the term 'rock and roll' to describe the kind of music he loved and played on his show."

The same teenage boy walked toward us again. John gave no indication that he noticed him. *He must have run around through the park to get ahead of us so he could see John again,* I thought. He didn't ask for an autograph, which was a shame. John would have given him one.

"Did you go to a lot of rock and roll shows?" John asked.

"I did. Alan Freed's shows drew big audiences even though the early ones were pretty primitive," I replied. "The artists were usually black doo-wop groups like The Harptones, The Cadillacs, The Cleftones. They didn't have backup bands. Alan Freed had a house band on stage to accompany them. Red Prysock played tenor sax. There'd be drums, bass, and one or maybe two guitars. Each group would come on stage and usually sing two songs. Then the next one would come on. Freed also was in several rock and roll movies in the '50s. At some of Freed's shows they'd play the movie and then have the stage show. Chuck Berry was in several of the movies." I paused. "I even saw Elvis live."

"You did?" John said, excitedly. "Where? Tell me about it. Elvis was my idol. When I heard 'Heartbreak Hotel,' that was it for me. I wanted to be like Elvis. That's when I formed The Quarrymen. What was his show like?"

"It was 1957, a year or so after 'Heartbreak Hotel.' I was living in a dorm at Fordham University in the Bronx. It was my sophomore year. I saw a newspaper ad that said something like 'Only Eastern Appearance. Elvis Presley at the Arena in Philadelphia.' He was wildly popular then, remember? The tickets cost $2.00, $2.75, and $3.50."

"That's all?" John asked.

"Yup. So I sent for two $3.50 tickets right away. He was doing two shows on April 5 and two on April 6. My tickets were for the 7:00 PM show on April 5. I couldn't get anyone in the dorm to go with me. Nobody would go."

John was amazed.

"No one would go with you? So you went alone?"

"Yes. I'd never been to Philadelphia. I took the subway to the Greyhound Bus Terminal on Eighth Avenue and Fiftieth Street, across from the old Madison Square Garden, and boarded a bus to Philadelphia. When I got there I got directions to the Arena on a subway. I sold my extra ticket for $3.50.

"The Arena was a minor league ice hockey arena," I continued. "It wasn't very big. Maybe it held six thousand people but surprisingly it was only about half full. But my ticket was on the right side in the first row of a narrow balcony that ran around the room, looking directly down on the stage. A great seat.

"There were rows of police sawhorses on the floor blocking the stage. Policemen were lined up near the stage. The Jordanaires came on first. Then Elvis, holding his guitar, joined them. The crowd went wild. He was dressed in a black silk suit, a black shirt, and what looked like white bucks. I didn't think to bring a camera. Not even sure I owned a camera. There was merchandise, Elvis buttons, and other stuff for sale. I wasn't interested in that. I just wanted to see Elvis.

"The Arena was charged with electricity. Lots of very loud screaming. Elvis played for less than an hour— 'Heartbreak Hotel,' 'Blue Suede Shoes'—the songs from his early records. He ended with 'Hound Dog.' And that was it. No encores. Then an announcement, 'Elvis has left the building!'

"I retraced my route to the terminal and bused it back to New York. Don't remember what time I got back to the dorm. It was an exciting adventure. My roommate thought I was crazy. But there was no way I was going to miss Elvis when he was so close to New York."

"Sounds like something I would have done," said John. "This was before Elvis went into the Army?"

"It was. I think he went into the Army about a year later. This was the real Elvis, as real as he was going to be at that point in his career. He'd already made a couple of movies but I wasn't interested in his movies. The show I saw was before Colonel Tom Parker, his manager, exploited him—Las Vegas, all the glitter."

John peppered me with more questions about that Philadelphia trip. Seeing Elvis live in 1957 was important to me but not as important as it would have been to John. If he'd been able to see Elvis live, the performance would have been a milestone in his life. John was sixteen when I saw Elvis in April 1957; he didn't meet Paul McCartney until July that year.

I turned around to walk back to my office.

"Jay, next week on Friday, I'm performing at a tribute to Sir Lew Grade at the New York Hilton," John said. "Would you like to come to the sound check I'm doing that afternoon?"

"I'd love to," I said. "Who's Sir Lew Grade?"

"He's a big British TV entertainment figure," John explained. "I agreed to play a couple of songs at this dinner. I'm not crazy about doing it but, well, it's next Friday. I'll be singing two or three songs. I'll let you know the details. I'll see you then."

I thanked John.

The following day I served John's answers to the New York and federal court complaints.

Chapter 8

John's Last Live Performance

April 18, 1975
Grand Ballroom New York Hilton
New York City

JOHN CALLED ME A FEW DAYS BEFORE THE APRIL 18 EVENT,
which was being held in the Grand Ballroom of the New York
Hilton Hotel.

"Are you still interested in coming to my sound check for
the Lew Grade dinner?" he asked.

"I am. I've been thinking about it. Thanks for remembering."

"Oh no, I'd like you to be there," John said. "You can tell
me what you think about my performance."

"Thanks, but I'll just watch," I replied, laughing. He told
me how to pick up my backstage pass at the ballroom entrance.
It would permit me to come to his dressing room.

When I arrived Friday afternoon, John introduced me to
the band that would accompany him that night.

"This is my lawyer, Jay Bergen," he said. "This is my band
for tonight's performance. They're called BOMF, which stands
for Band of Motherfuckers. Jay's a rock 'n' roller."

For that night's august occasion, however, they were billed
as "John Lennon, Etcetera." I shook hands with all eight band
members. I knew John had met them at Record Plant. Their
heads were shaved and they had donned masks of faces on the
back of their heads. John had arranged for the masks to be
made. They were all dressed in black jumpsuits. John was wear-

ing a red jumpsuit. I wondered, *Why the face masks and the red jumpsuit?* Being just an observer, I decided not to ask too many questions.

After they tuned their instruments, I followed John and the band to the Grand Ballroom. I stood off to the left while the band assembled onstage. They ran through a couple of rough versions of their three-song set featuring "Slippin' and Slidin'," "Stand By Me," and "Imagine." John made suggestions during each song. Then he asked the band to perform the set once more straight through.

"It sounds good," he said when they finished. "I think that's enough." They left the stage and headed back to the dressing room.

At least two BOMF members went on to have long rock and roll careers. Mark Rivera, the sax player, has played with Billy Joel for decades. Vinnie Appice was Black Sabbath's drummer for years and has played in other bands.

I was beginning to realize that John's creative endeavors often had a deeper meaning. I learned later that, although he had agreed to play at the Salute, he would make a few points while doing so.

One was the two faces idea, aimed directly at the evening's honored guest. In 1969 Sir Lew Grade's company, Associated Television (ATV), had acquired a controlling interest in John Lennon and Paul McCartney's music publishing companies, Northern Songs and Maclen Music.

The lyrics of the first two songs John sang also contained subtle messages to Sir Lew. The first song, "Slippin' and Slidin'," the B Side to Little Richard's 1956 hit single, "Long Tall Sally," contained the following lyrics:

> *Slippin' and a-slidin',*
> *Peepin' and a-hidin' . . .*
> *I won't be your fool no more.*

Oh big conniver
Nothin' but a jiver . . .
Won't be your fool no more.

The second song was "Stand By Me," Ben E. King's 1961 hit. Its lyrics also seemed to fit the night's honoree:

No matter who you are, no matter where you go in life
You gon' need somebody to stand by you.
No matter how much money you got or the friends you got
You gon' need somebody to stand by you

Both songs were on *John Lennon Rock 'n' Roll.*
The final song was John's real message, "Imagine." Changing the lyrics to his big hit, he sang:

Nothing to kill or die for
*And no **immigration** too . . .*
No need for greed or hunger
*A brotherhood **and sisterhood** of man* (emphasis added)

Substituting "immigration" for "religion," John obviously referenced the Nixon Administration's efforts to deport him back to England. Only months later that case would be resolved in his favor. He inserted "and sisterhood" in the lyric "a brotherhood of man," I assume, to highlight equal rights for women.

I chatted with John for a few minutes in the dressing room.

"Thank you for inviting me to the sound check, John," I said. "I really enjoyed it."

"You're welcome," John replied. "I thought you'd find it interesting. Last time I was on stage was with Elton last Thanksgiving. I didn't want to do that, but it was fun. I'll talk to you soon."

That night, April 18, 1975, John Lennon gave the last live performance of his life.

Chapter 9

Facing Down Levy

May 6, 1975
330 Madison Avenue
New York City

JOHN AND I MET IN MY OFFICE ON MAY 5. I prepared him for his deposition by Levy's lawyers the next day. I told him that the only lawyer representing Levy I had dealt with was Alan Kanzer, who was six years my junior in terms of experience. I assumed Kanzer would be asking the questions.

I also explained that Barrett Prettyman, representing Capitol/EMI, and George Grumbach, representing Apple Records, would be present. I told John that Levy might be there, too. Of course there'd be a court reporter as well.

"Court reporters are trained to take down everything they hear unless the attorneys agree to go off the record," I told John. "So if you want to ask me a question, we can do that quietly or take a break to step outside the room."

John was relaxed and looking forward to the deposition. So was I.

"It'll be interesting if Morris is there," John said. "Have you met him, Jay?"

"No. What's he like?"

"He's a big, husky guy, over six feet tall. His voice is raspy like he's got a cold. He has a real New York accent. Morris can be quite charming. Loves to talk about himself."

"Answer only the question asked," I said. "Don't volunteer information. That will often give the questioner some new avenue to pursue. The easiest way to avoid doing that is to listen carefully to the question and answer only that question as briefly as possible. If you can answer it with a 'yes' or 'no,' that's fine. If you truly don't remember something, simply say so. Nothing wrong with that. You'll have an advantage over Morris Levy."

"What advantage?" John asked.

"You'll be telling the truth," I said. "Morris is going to lie because the allegations of the complaints tell a completely different story than the facts you, Harold, and May have related to me. It makes no sense that John Lennon, an artist knee-deep in written agreements negotiated by your favorite people, advisers and lawyers, would ever make an oral agreement with Morris Levy. To say you'd make one at a meeting in a bar/restaurant the first time you met him would be very hard to believe!

"I assume Kanzer will begin by asking you about the 'Come Together' settlement agreement and then go into the Club Cavallero meeting," I continued. "You've told me the facts about those two events several times. The band trip to the farm and your trip to Florida will undoubtedly come up. Just stick to the facts as you remember them."

"I can do that," John said.

The next morning at 9:30, John and I met at my office. We walked down to Kanzer's office on the west side of Madison Avenue at Forty-Third Street. When we entered the large conference room, we met Kanzer and Diamond. Kanzer was a young, short, thin man who wore glasses. He had graduated from law school in 1968.

What interested me most was why Kanzer was taking John's deposition instead of William Schurtman, who had been at the January 30 meeting. Surely Schurtman would be Levy's lead lawyer at trial. He should have been the lawyer to question John Lennon, the main defendant in the cases and the most important witness from Levy and Schurtman's standpoint. *Does Morris Levy not want to pay the higher hourly rate for Schurtman's time? Is that the reason he isn't here?* His absence made no sense to me.

I introduced myself to Morris Levy and Phil Kahl, Levy's gofer, who'd been at the Club Cavallero meeting. John said hello to them. They sat directly behind Kanzer and Diamond in chairs against the wall.

We also introduced ourselves to Prettyman, his associate, Michael Michelson, and Grumbach. Sol Granett, who we'd met at the February meetings, was also there. John and I were seated directly across from Kanzer and Diamond. The court reporter sat at the end of the table to John's left, facing him. The other defense lawyers were seated down the table to my right.

The deposition went smoothly except for the fact that Levy repeatedly made a face or rolled his eyes at many of John's answers. Finally, Kanzer asked the following series of questions:

```
    Q Did he [Levy] discuss whether you
might rehearse any of the selections
you were considering for the Rock 'n'
Roll album?
    A He wanted me to go to the farm and
I wanted to stay and rehearse and after
a few discussions on it I finally agreed
to go and rehearse there.
    Q Did you invite any musicians to
accompany you?
    A I didn't invite them. Mr. Levy in-
vited them.
    Q Do you recall the identities of
the musicians who --
```

Disgusted with Levy's behavior, I interrupted.

```
    MR. BERGEN: Mr. Kanzer, if Mr. Levy
is going to continue to grimace and make
faces every time Mr. Lennon answers a
question, I am going to have to ask that
he leave the room.
```

        MR. KANZER: I don't believe Mr. Levy
is doing anything improper.
        MR. BERGEN: You have your back to
him but I am looking right at him and
I will not permit the deposition to go
forward if every time Mr. Lennon answers
a question, Mr. Levy makes a face.

Kanzer and I went back and forth without any progress
toward a resolution of the problem. I upped the ante.

        MR. BERGEN: I am telling you right
now [Mr. Levy's conduct] hasn't been
proper as far as I am concerned and I
will not put up with it much longer. If
it doesn't stop, we'll get up and walk
out.

Levy stopped misbehaving. John's deposition continued
until the lunch break.

Chapter 10

John Sightseeing Grand Central Terminal

May 6, 1975
Grand Central Terminal
New York City

WHEN WE GOT DOWNSTAIRS I HAD AN IDEA.

"John, let's go to the Oyster Bar in Grand Central Terminal for lunch," I suggested.

"I've never been in Grand Central Terminal," John replied.

"You haven't? Then you're in for a real treat," I said. "It's a beautiful building, one of the most beautiful in New York."

We walked one block east on Forty-Third Street and into the Vanderbilt Avenue west entrance of Grand Central, onto the west balcony. The view across the vast expanse looking eastward to Lexington Avenue is spectacular. We stood there while John took in the view—the high vaulted ceiling, gleaming floor, massive windows, enormous Kodak color photo ad covering part of the wall at the opposite end, and people hurriedly crisscrossing the floor below around the information booth.

"This is a beautiful room," John said. "The architecture is marvelous. The very high ceiling makes the whole room so dramatic."

I didn't say anything. We finally walked down the marble steps onto the terminal floor. We proceeded toward the round information booth in the center of the floor. I followed John as he took in the line of classic train ticket windows on the right side of the floor. We walked down the steps to the floor below and entered the Oyster Bar.

"Ask if we can sit against a wall," John whispered to me. I did. We were shown to a table against the south wall of the room. "Jay, would you sit with your back to the wall so I'm facing you?"

"Sure." Once we were seated two busboys came to the table and asked John for an autograph.

"Not while I'm eating," he politely explained. "When I'm done eating I'll give you an autograph." They thanked him and moved away.

"When was the terminal built?" John asked me as we read the large plastic white menu with black print.

"In the early 1900s," I replied. "It's called a terminal because the trains that bring commuters to and from north of the city end here, as do trains that go to other parts of the country. During the rush hours it's a beehive of activity."

"Has the restaurant always been here?" John asked. "The arched tile ceilings are amazing."

"As far as I know, it's been here from the terminal's beginning," I said. "Jackie Kennedy Onassis is very involved in an effort to prevent developers from destroying the terminal and replacing it with an enormous office tower. The battle to save the terminal began recently."

"That would be terrible, absolutely terrible," John said. "Why would anyone want to do that? The building is a work of art."

"It's called greed," I said. "You think Grand Central is beautiful. You should have seen Penn Station over on the west side at Seventh Avenue and Thirty-Fourth Street. That was an architectural wonder. It was torn down about ten years ago to make way for the new Madison Square Garden, an ugly round structure built on top of Penn Station's lower level where the ticket booths and train tracks are."

"I appeared with Elton John at Madison Square Garden last November," John said. "It was Thanksgiving night."

"That's it," I said. "How did that happen?"

"Elton and I are great friends," John explained. "He happened to be in the city last summer when I was recording *Walls and Bridges* at Record Plant. He stopped by the studio one night to say hello. He wound up playing piano and singing vocal harmonies on one of the tracks I was recording, 'Whatever Gets You Thru the Night.' Elton extracted a promise from me for doing that. I agreed that if the song reached No. 1 on the charts, I'd perform live with him. I never thought I'd have to do that. I didn't want to perform live with anybody. The thought frightened me.

"The album was released in September. 'Whatever Gets You Thru the Night' was the single. It hit No. 1. Elton called me. 'I want you to appear with me on Thanksgiving night at Madison Square Garden,' he said. I had to say okay. I flew up to Boston to see Elton's show there. I wanted to see how his show was organized. I hadn't been onstage in years. I flew back to New York with him.

"I didn't know it but Yoko came to the show," John went on. "We met backstage and talked for a while. That's what started the possibility we'd get back together."

"That's quite a story," I said. "Lots of 'ifs' in there."

I told John he'd handled the deposition questions very well.

"Your answers to Kanzer's questions about the two 7-1/2 reel-to-reel tapes were excellent," I said. I looked at my notes.

"When he asked you when you gave Levy the tapes, you answered, 'I don't remember. Before I finished.' Great answer.

"Then he asked if you had any discussion with Morris about why he asked for the tapes. And you answered, 'He just wanted to hear it.' You nailed that down later when you said you didn't remember when you gave them to Morris because you were 'still engrossed in the recording or finishing it.' So it's crystal clear that, from your perspective, the album was not finished at that point."

"You've also told me that you don't consider an album finished until you're in the cutting room," I said, "and even then you can still change things."

"That's right," John replied. "I'm always listening and

thinking about changes until the last possible minute. And even in the cutting room you have to be very precise because you could mess up the whole album at that point."

When we finished lunch John graciously gave autographs to the two busboys, our waiter, and the maître d'. We exited the restaurant.

"Do you know about the Whispering Gallery?" I asked John.

"What's that?"

I explained that because of the perfect arch of the gallery's ceiling, and the ceiling's Spanish tiles, two people could have a whispered conversation by standing in diagonally opposite corners and speaking directly into the corners.

"You stand here facing into this corner," I told him. "I'll stand in the diagonal corner across the gallery. Then I'll say something to you." I did. It worked perfectly. John thought it was great, so we had a brief conversation that way.

As we left the gallery, I suggested we walk up the ramp toward Lexington Avenue.

"Have you ever been in the Chrysler Building?" I asked John.

"No, I haven't."

"It has an amazing Art Deco lobby that you, as an art student, have to see." I looked at my watch. "We still have some time."

We crossed Lexington at Forty-Second Street. John loved the lobby. I told him it was built in the late 1920s. As we walked up Forty-Second toward Madison Avenue, we looked back at the building. John marveled at its Art Deco crown and spire.

The afternoon session began at 1:55. Levy did not return, but Kahl did. Kanzer spent a long time questioning John about EMI's exclusive contract with him and The Beatles. The more Kanzer asked, the clearer it became that Levy knew at the October 1974 Club Cavallero meeting, if not before, that "EMI would have the last say on everything." That's just what John testified to.

John also repeatedly denied that a TV promotion was Levy's idea. He also said he'd never even heard of Adam VIII.

"I don't think [Levy] suggested [TV], no," he testified. "I think he liked the idea of doing it." John was the one who first raised the TV possibility in that meeting.

The deposition ended at 4:30 p.m. John and I took the elevator down to the street and walked uptown on Madison Avenue.

"By repeating many of his questions, Kanzer succeeded in making Levy's case worse," I told him.

"Why do you say that, Jay?" John asked.

"Because you continued to give basically the same answers to his repetitive questions. You used somewhat different words but all resulted in directly contradicting Levy's version of events. His version is simply wrong. You're telling the truth and, no matter how many times and ways Kanzer asks the same questions, your answers are always the same. Do you see what I mean?"

"Yes, you're right," John said. "He repeated a lot of questions. He doesn't seem to be organized in how he asks questions."

"I don't think he has a lot of experience taking a deposition. I think he also ran out of ideas for questions."

"Why?"

"Because we ended at 4:30. You did a great job today," I said. "Tomorrow Kanzer will probably ask you more questions about the two tapes you gave to Levy and your *Rock 'n' Roll* album, what the differences are between them, why the *Roots* album damages your reputation, etc. These are topics we've talked about. You're prepared to explain why *Roots* is shoddy and why it can't be a high-quality album. It's impossible to accomplish that from a 7-1/2 ips tape, right?"

"Absolutely," John said. "There's no question about that."

"It's also not the same album, is it?" I asked.

"No, it's not. I can list the many ways the two albums are

different."

After a couple of blocks I hailed a cab and we both got in. John dropped me off at Fifty-Fifth Street and Madison.

Chapter 11

John Rebuts False Claims

May 7, 1975
330 Madison Avenue
New York City

JOHN ARRIVED AT MY OFFICE AT 9:30 THE NEXT MORNING. We walked down to Kanzer's office in time to resume the deposition at 10:00. Neither Levy nor Kahl were present.

Again, John's testimony was excellent. Some revealed interesting and humorous things about him. The best way to recount them is in his own words, straight from his deposition testimony.

Kanzer began by asking John why he invited Levy to Record Plant on October 9, the day after the Club Cavallero meeting, to listen to the Spector tapes. That day happened to be John's birthday.

"I think I was there because people at the Record Plant gave me a great big sandwich for my birthday, sort of a joke sandwich . . . I would remember the big piece of bread that the Record Plant staff put together . . .

"I am not a great one for celebrating my birthday but people around you always want to celebrate it so I go along for the ride, feeling very embarrassed, and everybody was there and I sort of smiled a lot and was hoping it would finish quickly."

When asked whether Morris Levy was a "personal friend," John gave an interesting answer.

"Well, that's putting it a bit strong you know . . . [he was] [a]n acquaintance. It takes a long time to set up a situation where one would call somebody a personal friend. I don't have that many that I put under that category."

Kanzer asked John whether he was a member of the Club Cavallero. His answer made me smile.

"I think I was honored with a card, yes. I tend, you know, if there is a card to be had, I will join. I like sort of the credit cards . . . I mean I go somewhere and I see them waving cards around and I say, 'Can I have one?' and I get one through the post. I am also a member of Peter Luger's [a famous Brooklyn steak house] and I have only been there twice."

He was asked about promoting the oldies album on TV.

"You see, TV is a major influence," John said. "I watch TV and I like it. I also watch how they sell records on TV . . . And the idea was forming in my head over the period of time that I started the album about what to do with it and how to package it . . . I started forth in my head that you could have a brand new record sold like it was already an oldie but goldie and I was interested in that concept."

On the subject of Allen Klein, John was blunt:

"Allen Klein lives in a dream . . . Klein's greatest statement is that no contract means anything and it can all be read 200 ways and you know that suited him. . . . "

When John was asked why he cut "Angel Baby," a Big Seven-owned song, and "Be My Baby" from *Rock 'n' Roll*, he had a ready explanation.

" 'Angel Baby' was my favorite song, there was something wrong with it, I had resung it to try to improve it but it never quite got there. The real problem with 'Angel Baby' was that every one of those 28 [live musicians playing at the same time] was out of tune and no matter how I resang it, I could never get in tune with any of them because they were all out of tune . . . there was too much time on each side of the album and you cannot get a good volume once you get past, say, 20 minutes a side. You begin to lose quality and volume, meaning that you have to turn the album up, you know, it gets very dodgy sound-wise, when you get past about 20, 21 minutes, and this album kept running into 25, 26 minutes a side."

Kanzer asked John the basis for his claim that Levy's *Roots* album damaged his reputation.

" . . . the lousy cover and the commercials that are put on the back of the album, which is something I would never have allowed, selling other products that I have nothing to do with, and the fact that the picture was a picture of me from 1967 or something like that, and it was an awful picture, an awfully cheap looking picture, and it was a disgusting kitsch [which is] [s]omething in bad taste, so bad it becomes a collector's item sometimes . . .

"All I know is he had . . . seven and a half [ips tapes] and a certain limitation as to what quality of master he can make from a seven and a half apart from the tracks being different and the order being different . . . the length of time on each side of the album is different. It's just a mechanical fact of life."

Kanzer gave John an excellent opportunity to explain how the master tape used to press *Rock 'n' Roll* varied from the two 7-1/2 tapes he had delivered to Morris.

"In more ways than I can describe . . . I tried to tell you a few of them already. There is a basic quality difference in tape that is an established fact of life as to [t]hat quality. The tape quality depends largely on the speed of the tape. That is a definite difference.

"The other differences will be the artistic decisions on how much or how little extra boosting, EQ'ing, bringing up the middle, bottom, top, et cetera, et cetera, that can be done to each track you run down to make the master wax. There is a difference in—those are the basic differences of a seven and a half [ips tape] and a fifteen [ips].

"You know, we have been over this so many times. There are track differences, running order differences . . . Morris Levy's album is like putting out the Broadway rehearsal for a show in which the director . . . can change his mind . . . the whole concept of the Morris Levy package is not my concept, so he has taken the rehearsal of a Broadway show and opened in Boston . . . It's like taking the rehearsal before the show is finished and opening it to the public and inviting all the critics in to watch the rehearsal."

John then described the final steps in producing a record album.

"You don't make final masters from rough masters. You make a new master. You see, you don't make a rough master and then copy that rough master and make a master. You take it direct from the 16 tracks again, from the mixes, the mixes are then put on a reel and *then when the final order [of the tracks] which is of paramount importance is decided,* then they can take the whole thing apart, put it together again, and then from that they copy the final master from which the wax is supposed to be made of, and then, even in the cutting room, one can copy certain tracks from the final master because of loss of quality or whatever, again in the cutting room, and then add them to the master so it's a never-ending process." (emphasis added)

Kanzer asked John who owned the performance copyrights to his albums.

"EMI," John answered. "They own everything."

Kanzer asked whether Levy offered John "any royalties for anything whatsoever."

"It wasn't up to him to offer me royalties," he said. "My royalties are signed, sealed and delivered way back and I don't discuss my royalties. If you are talking about royalties from records, I wish they were as loose as you are trying to make out."

Although I and the other defense counsel argued on the record about Kanzer repeating a question as to why "the 'Roots' album is of inferior quality to 'Rock 'n' Roll,'" John answered.

"Again? . . .

"Just look at the packages and let's not even go inside, what's on the record. . . .

"Look at it. I have never had a record that sold strange people's records on the back of my record as far as I remember. I mean it's just, you know, a cheap, shoddy edition of a John Lennon album and The Beatles or any individual Beatle would not let something that looked or smelled like this be anywhere near the public. [John was holding his *Rock 'n' Roll* album in one hand and the *Roots* album in the other, referring to *Roots* as the "cheap, shoddy" one.]

"This is worse than the albums that used to be put out with The Beatles' names before we finally got control of our covers . . ."

Kanzer questioned John about how his reputation was damaged as a result of the unauthorized *Roots* album. John restated his earlier testimony about other Adam VIII products, unrelated to him, being promoted on *Roots*.

"I consider it demeaning to have my product tied in with a bunch of old crap that Morris Levy wanted to sell on his album and that's damage enough for me. . . .

"[My reputation was also damaged by] confusion in the public's mind as to what was going on, in the critics' mind and the record business' mind as to which album to buy, which album was the endorsed album by me, and the damage of putting out crummy tracks in an order and displayed in a way which I would never have allowed under the sun. I would sooner have never put it out than have it out like that and it damaged my reputation as an artist, as a performer, and it damaged, no doubt, the sales of my own album by confusing the public with where and what album to buy."

At 12:35 p.m. Kanzer seemed to run out of questions. John's deposition was over. When we got down to the street, John and I walked east on Forty-Third Street one block, then north on Vanderbilt Avenue, and wound up walking north on the east side of Park Avenue. It was a beautiful day.

"It went very well again," I told John.

"Good, I'm glad you think so," John said. "It felt good. What happens next?"

"At some point soon we'll take Levy's deposition," I replied.

"I'm confident that the federal case will get to trial before the New York State case. Judge MacMahon has a very up-to-date calendar. At some point we'll meet with him and he'll set a schedule for ending discovery. He'll also schedule the various steps leading to an actual trial date."

"Do you really think the federal case will move that quickly?" John asked.

"I do."

"Good," John said. "I want to get this over with."

Chapter 12

Irish Ancestors at the Bull & Bear

May 7, 1975
Waldorf-Astoria Hotel
New York City

As we continued up Park Avenue, I said, "You hit all the points about the differences between the two albums and the reasons your reputation has been damaged. You were great. That was a disaster for Levy. And it'll be a road map for your trial testimony."

"Thank you," John said. "Spending time reviewing the facts with you was a big help. I was able to remember a lot of what went on even though I'm not good on dates. Dates seem to disappear for me as time goes on."

"Your testimony about credit cards and your birthday party at Record Plant with the giant hero sandwich was very funny."

"But it's true," he said. "People are always handing out credit cards or sending them in the mail. And I've never liked celebrating my birthday. All the excitement around me by other people isn't fun for me."

"How did you feel today? You seemed very relaxed."

"I was more into it today. Don't know why," he said. "I knew better what was going to happen, how Kanzer was going to ask questions. And he kept giving me openings to answer the way I wanted to and the way I believed would be helpful to us."

Suddenly, a middle-aged woman stopped in front of us.

"You're George Harrison!" she said to John, excitedly.

"Yes, I am," John replied. "Thank you very much." As we continued walking, John and I looked at each other and burst out laughing.

"Do you want to get some lunch?" I asked.

"Thanks, but I'd better go home," he said. "Yoko's spending a lot of time resting." We neared the Waldorf-Astoria.

"Let's get something to eat," John said, suddenly changing his mind.

"There's a good place in the Waldorf-Astoria called the Bull & Bear. It's like a pub."

"I've never been in the Waldorf-Astoria," John said.

"We'll go in the main entrance through the lobby," I told him. "The hotel is another Art Deco masterpiece." We took our time walking through the beautiful lobby. I pointed out the elevators to the Waldorf Towers. "I'll tell you about them when we sit down."

We went downstairs to the Bull & Bear. The maître d' was a tall middle-aged Irishman whose face lit up when he saw John.

"It's a pleasure to meet you," he said, reaching out to shake John's hand.

"Nice to meet you," John said. They shook hands. I asked for a corner table and pointed. He escorted us to it. I sat in the corner facing John and the room.

"My mother's father was born in Ireland," I said as we looked at the menu.

"Really? Where?" John asked.

"In Limerick," I answered. "He came over sometime in the 1890s. His name was Michael Tierney. He became a New York City policeman. He died when I was about two or three. Never went back to Ireland."

"My great-grandparents on my father's side came from Northern Ireland in the 1800s also but earlier than your grandfather, I think," John said. "They landed in Liverpool."

"You had that book excerpt about the origin of the surname Lennon on the back of the *Walls and Bridges* insert. It's quite a detailed history of the origin of the name."

"I thought I'd throw that in as a bit of a joke, you know," John said. "Seemed like a lot more than anyone would really like to know about the Lennon name."

"My father's family was also Irish, I think," I added. "That grandfather's last name was originally spelled Bergin with an 'i.' His name was Peter. He was from Paterson, New Jersey. After my father was in high school, Peter changed the last name to Bergen with an 'e.' I don't know whether it's a true story but Peter got involved in a family hassle so he changed the spelling." John laughed.

"The Irish are great ones for holding grudges, they are," John said.

"Yes, Peter really fixed them, didn't he?" I replied, laughing.

The Bull & Bear has dark wood-paneled walls and a semicircular bar that backs up to the room's east end. It looks out onto Lexington Avenue. We sat on the side of the room bordering Forty-Ninth Street.

During lunch I told John some of the Waldorf's storied history.

"The Towers contain large suites and apartments that dignitaries and famous people occupied," I said. "Cole Porter, the songwriter, lived in the Towers for many years. In fact, he wrote one of his big hits, 'You're The Top,' and others in his suite. Some people own their suites. Others rent on a monthly or yearly basis."

"I know who Cole Porter is," John said. "That's a great song. He wrote a lot of great songs, didn't he?"

"He certainly did. I don't know whether you saw *What's Up, Doc?* Barbra Streisand sang part of that song in the movie. It came out a few years ago. Ryan O'Neal and Madeline Kahn were in it. It's very funny. The opening sequence is hilarious."

"I didn't see it," John said.

As we ate we talked about the case.

"We're going to have to do some explaining about all the time you spent with Levy," I said.

"Is that going to be a big problem?" John asked. "I thought that once Harold and I told Morris that we needed EMI's permission to sell the album on TV, that was the end of the discussion. We'd have to wait until the album was finished before we brought up the TV idea to EMI. When Morris started talking about it when we were together, I stopped him. 'That's not my department,' I'd say or something like that. He finally stopped bringing it up."

"I understand," I said. "It's not a big problem. It's just another factor we'll have to deal with at trial. Your deposition testimony was very good. You made our key points very clearly. Morris was told about EMI, he knew about EMI, and you and Morris were not pals or mates, period. The farm weekend was a way of Morris showing you off, to put it crudely. You didn't want to go; he twisted your arm until you gave up. You went to Florida because it was something to do with Julian. Morris arranged for someone to loan you, May, and Julian the condo you stayed in, right?"

"Yeah, I think it was his friend Lew Garlick's condo at Sun and Surf or his daughter's," John said. "And again there were always lots of people, I guess friends of his or Morris's, hanging around. I got tired of that so I spent a lot of time in my room. And then Harold and I had to review The Beatles' partnership dissolution papers. That was a pain in the neck."

"That's fine," I said. "You can explain it just like that because you'll be asked about that at trial. There's an honest explanation for the fact that you were with Morris at the Club Cavallero and in Florida. You'll be fine with that. Okay?"

"Well, that's the way it was," he said.

After lunch John gave the maître d' an autograph.

Chapter 13

Dangerous Levy

June 1975
430 Park Avenue
New York City

I KNEW MORRIS LEVY WAS CONNECTED TO THE MAFIA AND THAT AN ALLEGED BUSINESS PARTNER, Thomas Eboli, had been assassinated. I didn't know whether he was really dangerous. Now we, the defendants, were going to take his deposition.

Kanzer defended Levy at the deposition in our office. Again I noted Schurtman's absence. Also present were co-counsel, Prettyman and Grumbach.

Levy's answers to my questions could well have begun with the words "once upon a time." His version of the October 8 Club Cavallero meeting with John was completely different from John's. The operative words, allegedly quoting John Lennon, seemed to be "we have a deal," which Levy kept repeating.

The purpose of a pre-trial deposition is to learn as much as possible about what a witness knows about conversations, documents, and events related to the lawsuit. Another purpose is to "freeze" the recollection of a witness so he can't tell a different story at trial. If a witness does tell a different story at trial, he leaves himself open to damaging cross-examination.

I decided to let Levy know I had checked into his background. I asked him if Thomas "Tommy Ryan" Eboli had ever been a partner in Roulette Records or other companies he controlled. Levy stared at me intently. His face flushed. He got up from his chair, glared at me, and left the room. I looked at Kanzer.

"What's going on?" I asked. He didn't respond but followed Levy out of the room.

Obviously Kanzer did not know who Thomas Eboli was or anything about his possible connection to Levy, who would later become the model for Hesh Rabkin, the Jewish music industry gangster in the enormously popular television show *The Sopranos*. Rabkin owned a horse farm, as did Levy. Ten minutes later Kanzer and Levy returned to the room and sat down.

"I suggest that you pursue another line of questioning, Mr. Bergen," Kanzer said. Feeling I had made my point, I switched to topics relevant to the case.

The deposition continued into the next day when Prettyman and Grumbach questioned Levy.

On June 26 I learned from a *New York Daily News* article just how dangerous Morris Levy could be. A day earlier Levy and Nathan McCalla, his bodyguard, had been indicted by a New York County grand jury on assault charges. The indictment charged that on February 26, 1975, McCalla pinned New York City Police Lieutenant Charles Heinz's arms behind him while Levy punched the plainclothes officer several times in the face. Allegedly, Levy was leaving a Manhattan restaurant with a lady friend when Lieutenant Heinz remarked to her, "You're a beautiful young woman." The comment angered Levy. With McCalla and Levy at the time was Levy's very close friend, the Rev. Louis Gigante, a Roman Catholic priest and the younger brother of the Mafia boss known as "The Chin," Vincent Gigante.

As a result of Levy's brutal assault, Lieutenant Heinz's left eye was removed several days after the incident. Many months after the indictment, their criminal case mysteriously disappeared from court records before they were brought to trial. A civil suit filed by Lieutenant Heinz was quietly settled out of court. Justice was served in a New York City way.

This scary incident occurred one week after Big Seven and Adam VIII issued their February 19 New York Supreme Court summons and complaint against John and the other defendants.

Levy was truly a dangerous mobster, but I never told John any of this information. Given John's worldwide fame, I didn't believe Levy posed any danger to him.

Chapter 14

A Pipe Dream

July 15, 1975
US District Court
New York City

WE HAD OUR FIRST PRE-TRIAL CONFERENCE BEFORE Judge MacMahon in a large wood-paneled courtroom in the US Courthouse on July 15. As the judge assigned to the case, MacMahon would use the conference in two ways—to discuss some of the factual and legal issues and to set the schedule we would follow leading to the trial.

The judge was in his mid-sixties: he had dark partially graying hair and bushy dark eyebrows. He sat at a table in front of the judge's bench. When our case was called, we sat across from him.

For the first time, Schurtman appeared on behalf of his clients. He was short, stocky, and about five or six years older than me. Kanzer accompanied him.

We explained to the judge that, to simplify matters, we had agreed that all pre-trial discovery would apply to the New York Supreme Court case and this one. MacMahon was all business. He had read the complaint and the answers and counterclaims. He knew the details of the parties' factual and legal positions.

As we brought the judge up to date on the pre-trial proceedings, he interrupted Schurtman, telling him that his clients' $14 million damages claim was a "pipe dream." Schurtman replied that the plaintiffs had a valid basis for their antitrust claim, but the judge was obviously not impressed. Judge Mac-

Mahon's comment was very interesting but did not surprise me. It wasn't unusual for the judge, who had a reputation for brutal frankness, a short temper, and a belief that cases should be presented expeditiously. His goal was to narrow the issues before him and move the case to a speedy conclusion.

He gave us only three months—to October 15—to finish all discovery matters. He also told us we could possibly have a trial date before the end of the year. All good news.

I told David Dolgenos and Harold Seider on a conference call what had happened. Later that day I also told John about the conference, noting that Judge MacMahon had told Schurtman, making his first appearance, that the plaintiffs' $14 million damages claim was a "pipe dream."

"Is that good for us?" John asked.

"Judges sometimes make offhand remarks like that," I replied. "However, when Judge MacMahon speaks, he means what he says. He knows when a claim doesn't make sense and is not shy about saying so. Levy is not going to like that."

The following Monday, July 21, Harold called to tell me Levy had proposed a settlement. The night of Judge Mac-Mahon's pre-trial conference, Levy had called Mike Lipton, a United Artists Records executive and a colleague of Harold's. Levy proposed a settlement to Lipton, whom he knew through prior business dealings: The defendants would pay Levy's legal fees to date. Capitol/EMI would license the master recording of *Rock 'n' Roll* to Levy for sale on television. Levy asked Lipton to pass the proposal on to Harold.

Levy's proposal amounted to John and Capitol/EMI totally capitulating to him.

"I told Mike to tell Levy he started the litigation and it's out of my hands," Harold said. "I can't discuss a settlement since EMI owns the master to John's album. Only they have the right to license it."

"Amazing," I said. "Morris must be in a panic about Judge MacMahon's 'pipe dream' statement and the fact we could have a trial by the end of the year. He told you, 'I got a shot. I got a shot.' Now he's not so sure, is he?"

"No, he's not," Harold replied. "I agree."

The offer confirmed to me that when Levy filed the lawsuits, he'd been gambling that John would settle and that he'd be able to wangle a deal with Capitol/EMI. They were a planned bullying tactic before *Rock 'n' Roll* was even released.

I called John about Levy's proposal. "This happened within hours of Judge MacMahon's $14 million 'pipe dream' remark," I said. "He's on the run, John."

"It sounds like he's worried," John said. "He knows I didn't make a deal with him that night at the Club Cavallero, but Yoko and I are still very worried about Levy's cases."

"I understand. I'm confident you and our other witnesses will be impressive," I said. "I believe that Morris will not be a good witness. He has to lie. He's not going to be able to keep his story straight in front of a jury. He was not a good witness on his deposition."

"I hope you're right, Jay," John said.

On August 7 Levy's desperation became more obvious. Schurtman's firm filed a motion in the New York Supreme Court case requesting a "general trial preference." It was an attempt to have the court move Levy's case ahead of other cases on the court's calendar, some of which had been pending for many more months or possibly years. They wanted a quick trial before Judge MacMahon's could begin. However, Levy's affidavit in support of the motion contained no reason for the court to grant such extraordinary relief.

We filed papers opposing the motion, pointing out the plaintiffs had no factual or legal basis under New York law for being granted a "general trial preference." We added that pretrial discovery in the almost identical federal case against the same defendants would end by court order on October 15, followed shortly by a trial. The New York Supreme Court shelved Levy's motion. There was nothing more Levy could do to avoid a trial before Judge MacMahon.

Chapter 15

John's *Rock 'n' Roll* Band

BOB GRUEN

From the left, Jesse Ed Davis, Eddie Mottau, Klaus Voormann, Jim Keltner, John,
and engineer Shelly Yakus in the control room at Record Plant, October 1974.

November 1975
Los Angeles and Detroit

In October Judge MacMahon granted a motion
by Levy's legal team to extend the discovery deadline to
November 14.

At the same time I decided I'd need one or more of the
musicians who played on the album to testify about the farm

weekend. In his deposition, Levy had testified there was talk that weekend about John doing the oldies album for him and his company to sell on TV. John told me he'd never had those conversations at Levy's farm or anywhere else. I had to find out what the musicians remembered.

On October 9, John's birthday, Yoko Ono gave birth to Sean Taro Ono Lennon. After an appropriate time had passed, I called John.

John, Sean, and Yoko, November 1975   BOB GRUEN

"Congratulations, John, to you and Yoko," I said. "You must be deliriously happy."

"We are very, very happy," John said. We chatted about how Yoko and Sean were. "I'd like to come up to talk about an idea I had to interview the *Rock 'n' Roll* musicians," I said. "I may want to use one or two to testify about the weekend at Levy's farm."

"Why would we need their testimony?" John asked.

"Levy's going to argue that you and others talked at the farm about doing the oldies album for him to sell on TV," I replied. "That's what he claimed in his deposition. He testified that he rented the drum kit and other things for the rehearsals.

He paid to bring the musicians up to the farm and supplied the food and drinks. We have to be able to rebut any evidence to support his claims. I also have a gift for Sean."

"You're right," John agreed. We set a meeting time in a few days.

When I arrived, John was beaming. I gave him the gift my wife had bought, an outfit that would fit Sean in a few months.

"Thank you. Come into the kitchen," he said. "You can meet Sean and say hello to Yoko."

The kitchen was down a hall from the front door. It was a large room with a lounge area—a couch and a couple of chairs—at the east end. Sean was in a bassinet. Yoko sat next to it. Not wanting to overstay my welcome, I congratulated them and took a quick look at Sean.

"Let's go to the living room where we can talk," John suggested. I followed him. We talked about which musicians I wanted to speak to. "I'll contact them to tell them you want to speak to them. My office at Capitol can give you the details about the band."

"That would be great," I said. "I'll make arrangements to see them in Los Angeles as soon as possible."

Before I flew to Los Angeles on October 19, I realized I couldn't meet these rock 'n' rollers dressed in my lawyer's uniform, a suit and tie. I bought my first pair of cowboy boots. I added two Western-style shirts—one light blue, the other black. The latter had white trim around the cuffs of the sleeves and the pocket on the left side. I found a pair of black Levi jeans, which I ran through the washing machine a couple of times so they didn't look brand new. I was all set.

I met drummer Jim Keltner and bass player Klaus Voormann at Sunset Sound, an LA recording studio, on October 20. They were working with Ringo Starr and Harry Nilsson. Ringo and Harry were sitting at the sound board in the control room. After we introduced ourselves, they peppered me with questions about the case. They both knew something about Morris Levy's crooked reputation.

Jim and Klaus then came in from the studio. All of them, particularly Ringo, were worried about how John was handling the situation. I assured them John was fine.

"John's been a big help in preparing for the trial," I told them. "He's very relaxed and happy about Sean's birth. He made it clear he's not giving in to Levy's bullying. John's all set for the trial. It's a difficult case but they're all difficult in one way or another. John's our key witness. I think he'll be great. He did a terrific job when Levy's lawyer took his deposition in May."

Jim Keltner and I went out to the reception area. He was of medium build, about five-foot-ten, and had bushy brown hair. He was wearing sunglasses. Jim told me he had played on *Mind Games*, *Imagine*, *Walls and Bridges*, and *Rock 'n' Roll*. He had worked on all the Spector sessions in Los Angeles, too.

"The sessions were pretty wild with lots of musicians playing at the same time," Jim said. "May Pang called me last October. She told me John was going to use as much of the Spector sessions as possible and finish the album in New York by recording new tracks. She said they were going to rehearse at Morris Levy's farm.

"I don't know anything about Morris Levy," he added. "I didn't want to go to the farm because I don't like to rehearse. May said John didn't want to go to Levy's farm, but Levy kept insisting and John finally had given up. After we got to the farm someone may have mentioned to me—maybe one of the guys or May—about Morris trying to work out a deal with John to put the oldies album out on a mail order thing. John had apparently told Levy that he had to get EMI's permission to do that. I'm not interested in the business side of things. I was there to just play music."

I then interviewed Klaus Voormann in the reception area. Klaus was about six feet tall, thin with long wavy hair. He had known John since they met in Hamburg in 1960. They were good friends. A trained artist, he followed The Beatles to London after their Hamburg gigs ended. He played on the same Lennon albums as Keltner, except for *Imagine*. He hadn't participated in any of the Spector sessions.

"John asked me to design the *Revolver* album cover," Klaus told me. "We were all surprised when it won a Grammy in 1967 for Best Album Cover, Graphic Design.

"I'd never heard of Morris Levy," he continued. "May called me about finishing up the Spector tapes. She said they'd rehearse at Levy's farm the weekend before recording at Record Plant. May told me Levy may be involved in the album some way. They were going out to the farm because Levy kept insisting on rehearsing there and John got tired of saying no. John felt that Morris wanted him up there so he could show him off.

"John did tell me that they were going to finish up the Spector tapes and record several songs owned by Morris's publishing company. I thought that was the connection between John and Morris. I had a feeling that Morris was a friend of John's."

He hadn't overheard any discussions at the farm about a deal between John and Morris.

"I do recall John saying that Morris has lots of chances to sell things on TV. Maybe Morris would have something to do with this album. Sometimes John talks very loosely about business matters. He's naive about business. I thought it was very strange that John could do something with Morris because anything that John does would have to be done with Capitol. As far as I was concerned, the whole thing sounded very vague and didn't sound like an agreement.

"If people start talking about business, I turn off and walk away," Klaus added. "I didn't hear or talk to any of the guests about any business matters or about the record, only that we were there to rehearse and were going to do an album with John."

Later that afternoon I met Kenny Ascher, the keyboard player, at A&M, another recording studio. He was very friendly and outgoing. Kenny had played on *Mind Games* and *Walls and Bridges*. He hadn't played on the Spector tapes but knew about them. May had called him to play on the sessions that would complete the oldies album.

"I was in New York when May called me," Kenny said. "I was at the farm Friday and Saturday but left early on Sunday morning. There were no discussions that I heard or participated in about the album or how it was going to be marketed. I didn't know Morris Levy but I'd heard he had some interest in Roulette Records.

"I drove up to the farm with Jim Keltner," he added. "I didn't ask why we were going to the farm. I never heard the names Big Seven or Adam VIII over the weekend."

These interviews made it clear to me that session musicians were hired to play music. Their attitude is, tell me when and where I have to be and what I'm going to play. That's all they want or have to know. It's very simple: to them, it's just a gig.

Next I flew to Detroit, where I had tracked down Jesse Ed Davis, the lead guitar player, at a hotel outside the city. We met in his hotel room on October 21. Jesse Ed was on the road with Rod Stewart and Faces, the English rock group. Part Comanche and part Kiowa, he was originally from Oklahoma.

"I met John at the Rolling Stones' *[Rock and Roll] Circus* movie concert in London in, I think, 1968," Jesse Ed told me. "I played on the Spector sessions in 1973 and *Walls and Bridges*. At one point the sessions stopped in December. I heard that Phil had disappeared with the tapes. Phil was really crazy. One night he fired his gun at the ceiling in the studio's bathroom.

"May Pang called to ask me to come to New York to finish the album last October," he went on. "She mentioned that we were going to Morris Levy's farm to rehearse. I had never heard of him except as the co-writer of 'Ya Ya.' The rehearsing consisted mostly of listening to old records, the original versions of the songs we were going to record the next week. We all knew the songs. They were old classic rock 'n' roll songs. I got the impression that Morris Levy was involved because some of the songs were owned by him.

"Either May or Jim Keltner mentioned that maybe the album would be put out as a TV mail order album. That seemed strange to me because I knew John was with Capitol. That's all I heard about the album the entire weekend. There was a tremendous amount of food served and lots of drinking and good times. Morris had a lot of guests who sat at one big table and we sat at another table.

"I didn't talk to Morris much except to socialize. I beat him seven games in a row in backgammon. He got mad and wouldn't play with me anymore. One afternoon Jim Keltner and I borrowed a Winchester rifle and a pistol from Morris's gun rack. We went outside and shot apples off a tree. We got bored with that game pretty quickly. Morris's house was huge. So was the land around the house. I spotted a big pond out back of the house. There was a rowboat tied up to a small dock. I shot it full of holes, sinking it. We apologized to Morris but it didn't seem to bother him. That was it. We left on Sunday."

Jesse Ed was very bright, very articulate. I liked him right away. He had a great sense of humor, too. I thought he'd make a very good witness.

When I got to my office the next day, I checked something Jesse Ed had told me. He said the only reason he knew the name Morris Levy was because he was listed as one of the writers of the 1961 Lee Dorsey hit, "Ya Ya." Morris Levy owned the song and John had sung it on *Walls and Bridges* with Julian playing drums. Sure enough, Morris was listed as a co-writer of "Ya Ya." Another Levy royalty theft! I was confident he would not know an F-sharp from an A-flat.

I called John to give him a report about my interviews of Jim, Klaus, Kenny, and Jesse Ed.

"I want to use Jesse Ed as a witness," I told John. "He's very bright, has a great sense of humor. What do you think?"

"Jesse Ed's a great musician and very smart, but he loves to party," replied John. "I can personally vouch for that based on the time I spent with him during the Spector sessions. I'd bring him to New York early so you can spend time preparing him. That way you'll also be sure he's here when you need him."

"I'm going to interview Eddie Mottau by telephone since he lives in New Hampshire," I said.

"Eddie is a good idea," John replied. "I've worked with him several times. He's very reliable. You can count on him to make a good appearance."

After several phone conversations with Eddie I decided he'd be convincing about the farm weekend and the lack of discussion about any agreement between John and Levy.

While I did use Jesse Ed as a witness, before testifying he was involved in an interesting incident in January 1976 with Ronnie Wood, a new member of the Rolling Stones, and Mick Jagger. More on that later.

Chapter 16

Jay's Blunder

December 1975
The Dakota
New York City

By early December we anticipated a trial date as our case moved up Judge MacMahon's calendar.

The Capitol/EMI and Apple lawyers asked me to arrange a meeting with John before the trial. Prettyman and Grumbach had met John at his deposition in May. I delayed giving them an answer because I knew John didn't want to meet with anybody before the trial. I also knew he wouldn't come to our office so a meeting would have to be at the Dakota.

They kept pressuring me. I kept delaying until, finally, I got John's permission to hold the meeting. We all met in the drawing room at the Dakota.

When Prettyman began asking John questions, it became painfully obvious he was plowing old ground, so to speak. John stood up and looked at me.

"Why did you bring them here?" he asked, raising his voice. "We've been over this before in my deposition. This is a waste of my time."

"I'm sorry, John," I replied. "You're right." I looked at the lawyers. "We should go." When the elevator door closed, I turned to John.

"I'm sorry, John. I should have told them firmly: no meeting, it's not necessary and that would have been the end of it."

"It's alright, Jay," John said. "I understand they were pressuring you. Forget it."

We shook hands before I left. I promised myself I would never let that happen again.

One evening later that month, John asked me up to the Dakota to meet Tony King, formerly with Apple Records. Listening to the banter between John and Tony, a fellow Brit, made it clear they were old friends. John explained Tony had played Queen Elizabeth II in a TV ad they had produced for *Mind Games*.

"We might use it as a trial exhibit, along with the album jackets we chose," John proposed. He wanted me to see it. The three of us watched the ad in a small office in the apartment down the hall from the drawing room. The office, which was across from the kitchen, overlooked Central Park. There was a table and several plain wooden chairs. We huddled to watch a small TV on the table.

The commercial began with two doors opening, accompanied by a "royal" musical fanfare and a voice-over saying, "Ladies and Gentlemen, Her Royal Highness, The Queen." There was Tony, sitting on a throne, crowned and lavishly dressed in a flowing gown and beautiful red fur robe with white trim. He held a copy of the *Mind Games* album in his left hand and a scepter in his right. The red satin sash across Tony's chest read "*MIND GAMES*" in glittery silver letters. He praised the album in a high-pitched, elegant English accent:

"Good evening. I've been asked to do this commercial. It relates to a gramophone record called *Mind Games* by John Lennon." (See YouTube "John Lennon—*Mind Games* Advert.")

The ad was brief, brilliant, and hilarious. As we laughed, I leaned back in my chair. Suddenly its rear legs gave way. I flipped over backwards, landing on my back on the floor. John helped me up and then burst into laughter. Then we all laughed. My embarrassment quickly disappeared.

Since we were having so much fun, we decided to use the "Queen" ad in the trial, just to show how clever John's TV album commercials were.

Chapter 17

John Gets a Haircut

January 1976
The Dakota
New York City

ON DECEMBER 29 WE FINALLY RECEIVED WORD FROM Judge
MacMahon: our trial date was January 12. I called John immediately. He answered the phone.

"Happy New Year!" I said. "I just got word that the trial
will begin on January 12. The judge gave us two weeks' notice.
We should get together next week."

"Happy New Year, Jay," John said. "How do you feel about
this?"

"This is what we talked about. It's what we were shooting
for—a quick trial to keep pressure on Levy and his lawyers.
We're ready. All you and I need is some time to review the facts
one more time."

"You're right. I'll call you early next week."

True to his word, John called me on January 5. He asked
me to come up to the Dakota that afternoon. When the elevator door opened, he was holding the apartment door open. He
had a surprise for me.

"How do you like my haircut?" he asked, a slight smile on
his face. His long hair was gone. John had a crew cut. Smiling,
I answered as if I was not in the least bit surprised.

"Looks great, just great," I said. Then we both burst into
laughter. He was quite proud of his surprise. "When did you
get it cut?"

"A couple of days ago."

He'd had long hair when we met in February. His ugly, out-of-focus photo on the *Roots* album cover showed him with long hair. I didn't ask whether he cut his hair so it would look different for the trial. If John was asked on cross-examination, I had a feeling he'd have a good explanation. I'd be surprised again!

We sat in the drawing room and talked briefly about our respective Christmas celebrations.

"I have a ninety-minute commute from home to the office," I explained. "I'm going to stay at the Drake Hotel during the trial. It's around the corner from our office. That way I won't have to make that trip twice a day. I'll give you the contact info after I check in this Friday. Call me at the office or there in the evening if you have any questions. In the meantime, I'll be in my office all week. We should meet in my office around 8:30 next Monday morning so we can go to court together. Sound good to you?"

"That's fine," John said. I could tell from his demeanor he was relaxed and happy.

"I don't know what Judge MacMahon's courtroom looks like but he'll be in charge," I said. "He'll have a lot to do with picking the jury, which will probably be six jurors and two alternates. Levy's lawyer will make an opening statement. Then I'll make one, followed by Prettyman and Grumbach.

"The opening statement shouldn't be long," I said. "It's basically an outline, a road map, for the jury as to the evidence each attorney expects to introduce in support of his client's case."

"And then?" John asked.

"Levy's lawyer will call his first witness."

"Do you think I'll be called as one of Levy's witnesses?" John asked.

"I don't think so. That would not be the normal way to try a plaintiff's case. You'd call your important witnesses first to get the jury thinking about your proof. I assume Schurtman will present Levy's case. I've only seen him twice, though. He was at each one of Judge MacMahon's pre-trial conferences. He didn't take any of the depositions. Kanzer took them, as you know, and he defended all the depositions we took. I've never seen anything like this."

"What do you mean?" John asked.

"Schurtman didn't take your deposition. He should have," I said. "He didn't defend when I took Levy's deposition. He should have. You and Levy are the two key witnesses! If he's going to be the lead trial lawyer, how can he be thoroughly prepared? He had to be playing catch-up these last couple of months, reading deposition transcripts, reviewing documents, and so much more. It's a mystery to me."

John and I reviewed his deposition transcript. I was confident John would provide good testimony at the trial. I left the Dakota after reminding him to call me if anything occurred to him.

"I will," he said.

Chapter 18

Your Basic By-the-Book Judge

January 12, 1976
US District Court
New York City

JOHN CALLED AROUND MIDNIGHT ON SUNDAY, the night before the trial.

"Can Yoko come to the trial?" he asked.

"Of course," I said. "I'm sorry. I didn't think to invite her. She's more than welcome. I'm really glad she'll be there."

John and Yoko arrived at 8:30 the next morning. We met in my office with my colleague, Howard Roy. Howard had been working with me for several months preparing for the trial. John and Yoko were interested in what the trial would be like. We talked again about the first day. John was emphatic.

"I don't want to settle with Morris," he said several times. "I want him out of my life."

We went downstairs to John and Yoko's limo. Howard and I put our heavy trial bags, containing deposition transcripts and documents, in the trunk and got in the back seat with John and Yoko. We headed to the US Courthouse at Foley Square in downtown Manhattan, just north of City Hall and the Brooklyn Bridge.

"I like your tie. What's the story behind it?" I asked John. "I have a feeling there is one."

"I found it in a secondhand shop on Broadway. It's hand-painted," he replied. "It shows a butterfly trapped in a spider's web. I'm the butterfly trapped in Morris Levy's web. I'm going to wear it during the trial."

"It's great," I said. "Too bad you won't be able to testify about why you're wearing it."

Judge MacMahon's narrow, small courtroom had been converted from other space. There were several rows of benches for spectators separated by a middle aisle, all behind a low railing with a gate in the middle.

The jury box was on the right side, close to the two attorneys' tables. The plaintiffs' attorneys occupied the front table and the defendants' attorneys, the table behind it.

A low railing, with a gate toward its right side, separated the attorneys' tables from the judge's bench and several desks for court clerks and the court reporter, who would transcribe the trial testimony from the jury box. The witness chair was to the judge's left (the attorneys' right).

John and Yoko sat in the front row of the spectator section. The only other spectators were my mother, Helen, and my aunt, Helen Conlon. My mother had insisted on coming. She had never seen me try a case. But then I had never appeared in court representing John Lennon, the real reason for her attendance. I introduced them to John. He was very gracious and turned to Yoko.

"Yoko, it's Jay's mum and aunt," he said.

Yoko stood up and I introduced her. She and John were both very friendly. They thrilled my mother and aunt, who sat behind them. Thankfully, they didn't ask John or Yoko for an autograph.

We attorneys had a brief conference with Judge MacMahon in his robing room behind the bench—a small room with a desk for the judge and several chairs for the attorneys. The judge was friendly but direct in how he wanted to proceed. He decided immediately that the sole question to be tried first was whether Morris Levy and John Lennon had entered into an agreement. The judge said he would not permit us to present any other issues to the jury. His approach made sense: if the jury decided there was no agreement, the court would dismiss

Levy's other claims.

We returned to the courtroom. With the judge's assistance, we picked a six-person jury with two alternates. Schurtman then gave a meandering, repetitive opening statement that dealt with minutiae. He went on for forty-five minutes.

My opening statement and those of Prettyman and Grumbach were each fifteen minutes or less.

Schurtman's first witness was William Chapman, who briefly testified that he spent one night at Levy's farm during the weekend John and the band were there. He claimed that he stood in front of the fireplace, trying to get warm, when John approached and introduced himself:

"[He said], 'As long as we are here we should know each other's name.' I gave him my name, he gave me his. I asked him what he was doing there. He said, 'I'm making a record for Morris.'"

I could not picture John Lennon walking up to a complete stranger and introducing himself. Why would one of the most recognizable people in the world do that? I didn't cross-examine Chapman. I didn't want to give him an opportunity to expand on his testimony and somehow make it sound credible.

Schurtman then called Levy. He testified at length about his experience in the record and music publishing businesses. He'd barely begun testifying about the settlement agreement that resolved the "Come Together"/"You Can't Catch Me" copyright infringement case when Judge MacMahon declared the lunch recess.

Chapter 19

❖

Sloppy Louie's

January 12, 1976
Sloppy Louie's
New York City

W\E ALL GOT INTO JOHN AND YOKO'S LIMO.
"What would you like to eat?" I asked them.
"We're only eating fish," John replied.
I asked the driver to take us to the nearby Fulton Fish Market area on the East River. After a short drive, he stopped in front of Sloppy Louie's, an area landmark. It wasn't fancy in any sense of the word.

BOB GRUEN

Enjoying lunch at Sloppy Louie's are, from the left, Howard Roy, John (holding his butterfly tie), Harold Seider, Yoko, and Jay Bergen, January 22, 1976.

We were shown to a plain dark wood table in a corner toward the rear of the room.

"You didn't introduce yourself to William Chapman, did you?" I asked John as we read our menus.

"No. Why would I do that?" he asked. "Everyone knows who I am, what I look like. And, besides, I'm shy." Yoko smiled. Howard and I laughed. "I try to not be noticed. Morris's house was crowded with people I didn't know. He probably invited a lot of his friends to the farm because I was going to be there. If I leave my house to go out where there are people I don't know, it's usually for what I call 'business.' Otherwise, I'm home."

"I didn't think you would walk up to this man and say, 'Hi, I'm John Lennon,' and then say, 'I am making a record for Morris.' It made no sense to me," I said. "We should file that away. When you're testifying you may have an opportunity to tell the jury how ridiculous his testimony was.

"Did you and Yoko notice how the judge admonished Schurtman about asking immaterial questions?" I asked. They both nodded.

"He's exactly as you described him," John said. "No non-sense, no wasting time."

"Schurtman's going to have a problem because Morris likes to ramble when he's answering a question," I said. "He does not answer directly. He volunteers stories, not factual responses."

John and Yoko loved Sloppy Louie's. No one bothered us as we ate. John commented on the way back to court that he liked the delicious seafood and how casual and informal it was.

Chapter 20

Levy's Difficult Afternoon

January 12, 1976
US District Court
New York City

MORRIS LEVY'S AFTERNOON ON THE WITNESS STAND DID NOT GO WELL. He repeatedly volunteered testimony. I kept objecting. Many times Judge MacMahon asked Schurtman to just have the witness answer the question. It got so bad that the judge finally said to the jury:

> THE COURT: Ladies and gentlemen of the jury, you are the ones who will have to decide whether there was this agreement. That turns on what the parties said and on what they did, not on somebody's conclusion about somebody who was there.
>
> You have to know who said what, if you can decide whether there was an agreement or whether there wasn't.
>
> Please, hold the witness to conversations. We have been almost totally unable to do it, Mr. Schurtman.
>
> MR. SCHURTMAN: I respectfully disagree, your Honor. I think the witness --
>
> THE COURT: Please, I am not asking for your comments.

The judge adjourned for the day at 4:00 p.m.

We drove uptown.

"What did you think of today?" I asked John.

"It sounded like a bad day for Morris. Schurtman seemed to annoy the judge with some of his questions and Morris couldn't answer the questions directly. And the judge does not like it when Schurtman argues with him."

"You're right," I said. "Schurtman does not seem to know what kind of judge he's dealing with. He must not know anything about MacMahon's reputation. That's surprising. The judge is getting increasingly annoyed that time's being wasted."

"Morris's testimony was nowhere near what actually happened at the Club Cavallero," John said. "He was making things up about what Harold and I said. The TV thing wasn't his idea. I mentioned TV first because I wanted to avoid the critics."

"Yes, there's no question about that," I said. "You and Harold were both very clear about that in your depositions. Morris told one lie after another and his deposition testimony is going to trip him up when I cross-examine him. There was one very important thing he said that conflicts with a key allegation in the complaint about the terms of the agreement."

"His answer about the foreign rights didn't fit, did it?" Howard said.

"When Morris was describing what was said at the Club Cavallero meeting, he said there was a discussion with Harold about getting permission from EMI," I explained. "And Seider said he'd have to go to England to get this permission. Then Schurtman asked him what the permission was needed for and Morris answered, 'For the foreign rights.'

"That's a problem, isn't it?" I continued. "Every allegation they've made in the case from day one was that the agreement made at the October 8 meeting was for worldwide rights to sell the album. That means foreign rights. Today's testimony by Levy seems to be in direct conflict with their basic claim. He knew that John needed permission from EMI for the foreign rights. That's a very important admission."

We spent the rest of the ride talking about Levy's testimony on this point and how we could check it when we got the transcript later. I explained transcript protocol to John and Yoko.

"In a trial like this," I said, "the court reporters provide the attorneys for both sides and the judge in the evening with what's called 'daily copy,' the day's transcript, so it can be reviewed before the next day's testimony."

We had something to look forward to that night—reviewing the day's testimony. The limo driver dropped Howard and me off at our office.

Chapter 21

Swami's Prediction

Morning of January 13, 1976
Marshall Bratter Office and US District Court
New York City

WHEN JOHN AND YOKO ARRIVED AT MY OFFICE THE NEXT
MORNING, John said, "Yoko has something to tell you." I looked
at Yoko.

"I consulted my swami last night," she said. "He told me
that the trial would be interrupted today." I was nonplussed.
Her swami? I looked at John. He was looking at Yoko.

"What did the swami say?" I asked.

"He said the trial will be interrupted today."

"Yoko," I said, "we've got a judge who wants to move the
trial quickly, as we saw yesterday. We have a jury. We have witnesses flying in from London and Los Angeles. I don't see how
that can happen."

Yoko said nothing. John continued to look at Yoko and not
at me. Howard and I looked at each other as if to say, *Nothing
we can do about this.* There was silence in the room for what
seemed like a long time.

"We should get going," I finally said. The four of us proceeded downstairs and went into the limo.

The morning began with a conference in the judge's robing
room. Schurtman objected to a ruling Judge MacMahon made
the previous day about evidence Schurtman could not introduce:

```
THE COURT: It doesn't matter.
MR. SCHURTMAN: I think I am being
very seriously prejudiced by your
Honor's ruling.
THE COURT: You probably are not.
I think that's frivolous, totally frivo-
lous. You would like to run the trial
yourself, Mr. Schurtman.
MR. SCHURTMAN: No, I would simply
like to try my case --
THE COURT: Your way and not the way
the Court directs.
MR. SCHURTMAN: So I can present
material evidence.
```

Schurtman didn't seem bothered by butting heads with the judge. After we returned to the courtroom, Levy retook the witness stand. After a few more questions, Schurtman turned him over to me for cross-examination. He began volunteering information again, not answering my questions. I objected. The judge directed Levy to answer the questions and not volunteer. This pattern repeated itself multiple times. Then, after yet another improper answer from Levy, I objected.

```
MR. BERGEN: Your Honor, this is
all just volunteering. I didn't ask a
question to elicit this.
```

Judge MacMahon snapped. He lost his patience.

```
THE COURT: [Turning to the jury and
raising his voice] One of the things the
jury should do is, of course, judge the
credibility of the witness!
Go ahead. Don't volunteer.
```

Not long after that, Howard tugged at my jacket and pointed toward Schurtman. Lying in front of him on the table was John and Yoko's *Two Virgins* album. It was positioned to show the front of the jacket, which featured a nude photo of them.

Unfinished Music No. 1: Two Virgins was an experimental 1968 avant-garde album produced by John and Yoko. It contained no real music. EMI refused to release it. Apple Records released it in the US on Tetragrammaton Records. The US record and jacket were enclosed in a plain brown sleeve that covered John and Yoko's naked bodies except for an oval hole displaying their heads. The European *Two Virgins* had no brown sleeve covering the front and rear nude photos of them.

> MR. BERGEN: Your Honor, I would like to object to Mr. Schurtman laying out on the desk an album that I believe he has there in order to prejudice the jury and I would like to approach the bench.

I walked by Schurtman, picking up the album. The judge took the album from me and looked at the nude photo on the back cover. He tried to stuff the album into a round wastebasket behind him.

"Please don't throw it away," said Schurtman, now standing next to me. "I am going to use it in evidence, with your permission."

"Not in my courtroom!" the judge fired back.

Prettyman told the judge that Schurtman was holding the album cover so the jury could see it.

"Are you going to move for a mistrial?" the judge asked me. I consulted briefly with co-counsel.

"We move for a mistrial," I said.

"Granted," the judge said, apologizing to the jury and discharging them. "We will impanel another jury right away."

"May I make an application before we impanel—" Schurtman began. The judge interrupted him and said he was "mark-ing" *Two Virgins* as Exhibit 3-A. Before permitting Schurtman to make his application, he asked "for statements from the defense counsel . . . [a]s to what [we] could observe from where [we] were sitting."

Prettyman described how Schurtman had taken the album out of the brown sleeve, exposing the cover so that it was lying flat on the table. He picked it up and turned it around so the jury could see both sides. Then he put it down on the table.

"May I defend myself on that, your Honor?" Schurtman asked.

"Yes, you may say what you wish," the judge said. Schurt-man then gave a very suspect explanation as to why he was looking at the album while also denying that "it was in front of the jury." This was untrue. The jury box was only a few feet to the right of the end of the table where Schurtman was sitting and holding the album. The jurors could clearly see it. Schurt-man began baiting the judge.

They argued. The judge accused Schurtman of deliberately trying to prejudice the jury. Schurtman denied the accusation before falsely stating:

> MR. SCHURTMAN: Since the inception of this case, certainly since the confer-ence we had in the robing room when this case started, your Honor has indicated that you do not think we have much of a case. You have told me repeatedly that we have a weak case. You have refused to let me put in evidence —
>
> THE COURT: I never told you any such thing. You are an outright liar.
>
> MR. SCHURTMAN: Your Honor, if you think I am an outright liar then it is impossible for me to get a fair trial from you and I therefore request that

```
this case be assigned to another judge.
    THE COURT: I would be delighted to
assign it.
```

I objected to the case being reassigned.

```
    THE COURT: No. The rule in this court
is once we grant mistrials we automati-
cally reassign cases, because invariably
they are granted because of the miscon-
duct, the outrageous and foul misconduct
of a lawyer, which we saw right here.
```

The judge had never said any of the things Schurtman had accused him of saying in the robing room the previous morning or at any other time. The only comment Judge MacMahon had made about Levy's case was when he'd called the $14 million claim a "pipe dream" in July.

As the judge left the bench, I followed him and his law clerk into his robing room. This is not done.

"Your Honor, you can't do this," I said. "Now we don't have a jury or a judge."

"Mr. Bergen," he replied, "I'm sorry but Mr. Schurtman did this deliberately because his case was not going well."

I reentered the courtroom and addressed Schurtman and co-counsel.

"I'm going to see Chief Judge Edelstein," I said. Before I left I asked John and Yoko to wait for me.

When we all arrived at Chief Judge Edelstein's chambers, his secretary told us he was at lunch. I asked to dictate a memo to him.

"Sure," she said, picking up a steno pad and pen. I explained what had happened and added that the parties had witnesses lined up, some coming from out of town. I requested the appointment of a new judge as soon as possible. I thanked the chief Judge for his help.

Back in Judge MacMahon's courtroom, I explained to John and Yoko that "I just dictated a memo to the chief Judge telling him we had a mistrial and recusal by Judge MacMahon on the second day of a jury trial. I asked that a new judge be appointed as soon as possible."

"This is not good," Yoko said. "This should not have happened." John turned to her.

"Yoko, Jay's in charge."

"I'll call you as soon as I hear something," I said. "Don't worry. It's going to be alright. I think we'll get another judge soon."

John and Yoko went home. Howard and I had lunch with Prettyman and Grumbach.

So, the trial was interrupted!

Chapter 22

A Harpsichordist Judge

Late afternoon of January 13, 1976
US District Court
New York City

BACK IN MY OFFICE LATER, Pat handed me a message slip that read: "Come to Judge Thomas Griesa's courtroom as soon as possible."

I called Grumbach. He and Prettyman had gotten the same message. They were leaving George's office.

"Do you know anything about Judge Griesa?" I asked.

"I don't but I'll ask around the office for any info about him," he replied.

"Thanks, George." I called John.

"We've gotten a call to come to a judge's courtroom as soon as possible," I said. "We may have a new judge. I'll call you later."

"Good luck," John replied. Howard and I headed for the subway.

When all of us, including Schurtman and Kanzer, were present in the courtroom, a court clerk ushered us into the robing room. Judge Thomas Griesa introduced himself. He was about six feet tall, slender, and young. We introduced ourselves.

"Chief Judge Edelstein has assigned your case to me," he said. "I know nothing about the facts of the case. I don't know anything about John Lennon or The Beatles or Morris Levy. I have a case now, but the parties are in settlement negotiations. If their case settles we can begin your trial immediately.

"However, I have a suggestion. If both sides would agree to waive a jury, we could try your case on days when the other case is not on trial if it doesn't settle, or when I have time on my calendar if it does. We'd be able to take witnesses out of order and generally work around my schedule. Why don't you go out to the courtroom and confer? After you've made a decision, come back in. We'll talk."

In the courtroom we discussed the judge's suggestion among defense counsel. We decided we'd be better off without a jury. Why? Principally, we thought a judge who knew nothing about John Lennon or The Beatles would look only at the issues in the case. He'd make his decision on the facts. I thought we had the better position on the facts. I also believed John would be a much better and more believable witness than Levy.

I told Schurtman we were ready to tell Judge Griesa our decision. Defense counsel filed into the robing room first. I spoke before Schurtman had a chance to open his mouth.

"The defendants agree to waive a jury," I said. Judge Griesa turned to Schurtman.

"Well, Mr. Schurtman?" he said. There was a moment's hesitation.

"The plaintiffs and Morris Levy agree to waive a jury," Schurtman said. He may have thought the judge wouldn't be happy trying the case with a jury after we had agreed to waive one. Having a jury certainly would make the judge's daily calendar more difficult to handle. In any event, we got the jump on Schurtman by telling the judge the defendants' decision first.

Judge Griesa seemed pleased the issue had been easily resolved. He told us we'd begin the trial at 10:45 a.m. the next day.

I was happy. Schurtman's ploy to stop the trial before Judge MacMahon and delay a new trial, possibly for a long time, had backfired. It wasn't a setback for us.

By the time Howard and I got back to our office, there was

a message to call Grumbach. I called him back.

"Here's what I've learned about our judge," George said. "He's been on the bench about four years. He had been at Davis Polk [a large Wall Street firm] and is a bit of an egghead."

"What do you mean?" I asked.

"He's phlegmatic, very studious in the courtroom, asks lots of questions, kind of an intellectual," replied George. "Oh, and he plays the harpsichord and piano in a classical music group."

"What?" I said. "He's a musician? He plays the harpsichord? That's amazing. He and John can talk intelligently about music."

"You may be right," George said. "See you tomorrow."

I called John and summarized what had happened.

"I'm very happy with this result," I explained. "We haven't lost any time, really. We have a new judge and no jury. We'll start tomorrow at 10:45 a.m. We can take witnesses out of order and plan the presentation of our case the way we want to. What do you think?"

"What do you know about this judge?" asked John.

"He's young," I said. "He's only been on the bench about four years. He told us yesterday that he doesn't know anything about the issues in the case. He also said he doesn't know anything about John Lennon or The Beatles."

"Is that helpful to us?" John asked.

"Yes," I replied. "We can educate him and I know we can do a better job at that than Levy and Schurtman." I did not tell John that the judge was a musician. I wanted to tell him and Yoko in person the next day.

"Yoko and I are glad we're starting tomorrow," John said. "We're looking forward to this. We think it's great that we got another judge so quickly. Thank you for going to the chief judge."

Years after the trial ended, I learned that Judge MacMahon's chambers had called Rick Kurnit, Judge Griesa's law clerk, that afternoon and told him to come pick up the file on the Big Seven case. Kurnit hadn't been in court when we'd met the judge. When Judge Griesa returned to his chambers with his other law clerk, Susan Jackson, Kurnit joined them to discuss our case.

The judge's lack of knowledge about The Beatles, John Lennon, and their music apparently led to the three of them going to Ms. Jackson's apartment so she could play some Beatles and John Lennon records for the judge. By the time the trial began, Judge Griesa had heard at least some rock and roll.

Chapter 23

Levy Changes His Tune

January 14-15, 1976
US District Court
New York City

When John and Yoko arrived to pick up Howard and me, I shared what we'd discovered.

"Judge Griesa plays the harpsichord and piano!" I told them.

"Really?" John said.

"Yes, in amateur chamber music groups. We'll plan your direct testimony so it'll be a tutorial on The Beatles' and John Lennon's musical journey. It's important that he knows what you and the other Beatles have accomplished in the past fifteen years."

"Right," John agreed. "It'll be easy for me to communicate with him about music. That's wonderful that he plays the harpsichord."

"It's ironic," I said. "Thanks to Schurtman, we have a musician for a judge with no jury. You can take Judge Griesa through your work on *Rock 'n' Roll*. He's very calm in the courtroom, asks lots of questions, is a bit of an intellectual. This is what's called a bench trial, John. The judge is the sole finder of fact, no jury. This is good."

On the way downtown as we talked more about Judge Griesa's musical expertise, John changed the subject.

"Do you know anything about a singer named Freddie Mercury?" he said. "When I talk to Julian on the phone, he talks about Freddie Mercury. I have no idea who he's talking about."

"He's the singer and principal songwriter for Queen, a very popular British rock group," I replied. "They have a big album called *A Night at the Opera*."

"Their hit song is 'Bohemian Rhapsody,'" Howard added.

"I'd better learn more about Freddie Mercury so I can talk intelligently to Julian," said John, as we arrived at the courthouse. *John really has dropped out*, I thought. *He doesn't know who Freddie Mercury is.*

The trial began at 10:45 a.m. Judge Griesa reminded us to "assume that I don't know anything" about the facts.

"I would like to proceed in exactly the same fashion you were proceeding before Judge MacMahon," he said.

In other words, we'd try the breach of contract issue first.

After opening statements, Schurtman called Levy as his first witness. His direct testimony consumed the remainder of January 14 and all of January 15. He testified that TV promotion of the oldies album was his idea. John had testified in his deposition that he had mentioned selling the album on TV first.

Levy rambled for pages about what had been discussed that night at the Club Cavallero—John's royalties (John testified they were never addressed); Adam VIII, Levy's TV marketing company (John testified that the first time he heard the words "Adam VIII" was when he saw them written on the silo at Levy's farm, days after October 8); retail fulfillment centers (John had no idea what the term meant), and so on.

After pages of testimony about the meeting, Levy was suddenly enlightened by what I would call a "memory flash."

" . . . but there is something that I left out from backwards," he said.

```
     THE COURT: All right, you can go
back.
     THE WITNESS: There was some discus-
```

```
sion about getting permission from EMI.
    THE COURT: Who said what?
    THE WITNESS: Mr. Seider stated that,
I believe, that 'We got to get permis-
sion from EMI for the foreign for sure,'
he was not sure about the American
rights, if we needed permission or not.
    I then told Mr. Seider, 'You don't
need permission in the U.S. for mail or-
der with The Beatles' . . .
```

Levy testified that Allen Klein had told him that The Beatles did not need permission from EMI or Capitol for "mail order" sales—the kind where customers would see the TV ad, send in $5.98, and receive the record in the mail. Levy also testified he'd read the same thing in an Allen Klein *Playboy* interview. Levy was placing his reliance on a *Playboy* interview and on what Allen Klein, then engaged in bitter litigation with the three former Beatles, allegedly told him.

Pages later in the court transcript came another Levy "memory flash":

```
    THE WITNESS: Your Honor, as I am sit-
ting here something else came to my mind
that took place, too.
    THE COURT: All right.
    THE WITNESS: There was some discus-
sion, also, about Mr. Seider going over
to England to talk to Mr. Len Woods [of
EMI].

                •   •   •

    THE COURT: Let us not get vague about
it.
    THE WITNESS: No. That he definitely
```

```
know [sic] --
    Mr. Seider definitely said to me then
on the foreign rights he knew he had to
clear it with EMI . . .
```

These "memory flashes" were the same new "story" Levy
had told when testifying before Judge MacMahon. He had
now admitted twice in a matter of minutes that EMI would
have to give its permission before Levy would be able to market the oldies album on a "foreign" or worldwide basis. This was
a direct contradiction of Levy's initial claim, repeatedly alleged
in court documents, that he had the exclusive worldwide TV
marketing rights to the oldies album.

Levy also admitted that he knew, as did the entire music
industry, that The Beatles individually and as a group were
exclusively under contract to EMI and its subsidiary, Capitol.

When Levy testified that the meeting ended, Judge Griesa
pointedly asked him, "Did anyone say anything?"

Levy replied, "John Lennon said, 'We have a deal.'" *Huh?
John Lennon, a singer-songwriter who hates business, meets Morris
Levy for the first time, in a restaurant. John is there to explain the
delay in the oldies album. John tells Levy he's under an exclusive
agreement with EMI and then John says, "[w]e have a deal." Will
the judge buy that?*

"Boy, he sure can lie, can't he?" I said as we rode uptown.
"Levy's story about not needing permission for mail order is a
fiction. And how about John Lennon saying, 'We have a deal'?"

"Will the judge believe this?" John asked. "Business is not
my job. I wouldn't know where to begin. I can't make deals."

"I know," I said. "They seem to be abandoning their claim
that you agreed to a worldwide deal because they can't prove it.
We have Levy's deposition transcript, the two complaints, their
other court documents repeating the original worldwide claim.
They're stuck with that claim."

On January 15 Levy testified that John quickly agreed
to rehearse the band at his farm the weekend before October

21–25, when the band went into Record Plant to lay down new basic tracks to complete the oldies album. Actually, John very reluctantly agreed to "rehearse" at the farm. He didn't want to seem rude by declining Levy's repeated invitations.

Levy told a story about meeting John unexpectedly at the Club Cavallero in mid-November 1974. He said John and May were having dinner with "a part owner or engineer" from the Record Plant and his wife. [We were able to prove later in the trial that this "dinner" with John, May, and Roy Cicala, the Record Plant's owner and chief engineer, and his wife, Lori, actually took place in December, not November.]

According to Levy, John had said: "'It's finished. I'm buying him dinner. We all worked hard. I don't want to hear the damn thing again. I have had enough of it. I'm that way after I complete an album. I get to hate them after I complete them, because I have done nothing but listen to this for a few weeks now, and it is your baby.' At that point I suggested that I would like to have the tapes."

This was pure fantasy. John had testified at his deposition that before he finished work on the oldies album, Levy asked him for a reel-to-reel tape because he "just wanted to hear it." It was during "that period I was still engrossed in the recording or the finishing of it."

Barely one month after recording the basic album tracks, John would not tell Levy that "it's finished." The lie was transparent. John certainly would never hand two reel-to-reel 7-1/2 ips tapes to Levy and say, "it is your baby," with the intention they'd be used to manufacture an album. The industry standard was to use 15 ips tapes to manufacture major artists' albums.

Morris Levy's cross-examination began on Friday, January 16, but was not completed. Over the weekend the attorneys agreed to suspend Levy's cross-examination until later in the trial.

Chapter 24

Two Puerto Rican Girls

January 16-19, 1976
Drake Hotel
New York City

JESSE ED DAVIS FLEW TO NEW YORK ON FRIDAY, January 16. I
intended to call Eddie Mottau, Jesse Ed, and John as witnesses
the next week on Tuesday, January 20. I got Jesse Ed a room at
the Drake, where I was staying. When I returned from court
on January 16, I went to see him. We talked for a while about
his testimony and arranged to meet over the weekend.

While we met on Sunday, his phone rang. I heard Jesse
Ed's side of the call. It went something like this, "Yeah, yeah
man. That's fine. Cool. Sure. Yeah, I'll see you later."

"Who was that?" I asked.

"Ronnie Wood. The Stones are in New York finishing their
Black and Blue album. Ronnie's with the Stones now. We're
going to meet later." (I knew Jesse Ed and Ronnie had become
pals during the Faces tour the previous fall.)

"I'd appreciate it and so would John," I said, "if you would
not overdo the nightlife until you testify this week."

"No problem," Jesse Ed replied. "It'll all be fine. I'll be cool.
Don't worry." *I am worried*, I thought, *but there's nothing I can do
about it.* We set a time to meet on Monday.

When I telephoned Jesse Ed Monday, he gave me a different room number. He opened the door when I knocked. I
walked into a suite with a living room and bedroom off to the
left.

"What's the story with the suite?" I asked.

"Last night I brought two Puerto Rican hookers back to the hotel," he replied. "The night desk clerk and the house detective wouldn't let me take them to my room. They said my room is supposed to be occupied by only two people, not three. So they moved me to this suite."

"They moved you? All your clothes and everything?" I asked. "What time was this?"

"About four o'clock." I decided not to ask more questions.

A brief aside: In 1978 I was driving when the radio DJ introduced "Miss You," the single from the Rolling Stones' new album, *Some Girls*. It was Ronnie Wood's first album as a full-time member of the band. In the second verse Mick Jagger sings:

> *Been waitin' on your call*
> > *and the phone rings*
> *It's just some friends of mine that say*
> *"Hey, what's the matter, man?*
> *We're gonna come around at twelve*
> *With some Puerto Rican girls that's just*
> > *dyin' to meet you*
> *We're gonna bring a case of wine*
> *Hey, let's go mess and fool around*
> *You know, like we used to."*

It takes a few seconds but then it hits me. That was the night in January 1976 before Jesse Ed testified when he and Ronnie Wood were partying. They called Mick Jagger. He remembered the call when he wrote "Miss You." I don't know whether they went to his place but Jesse Ed wound up with the "Puerto Rican girls."

Back to Jesse Ed in his Drake Hotel suite. We sat down to talk. I explained that Eddie and he would testify the next day, followed by John. The phone rang. I listened to basically the same conversation I'd heard the night before with Ronnie. I didn't have to ask who it was.

"Hey, take it easy tonight," I told him. He assured me everything would be fine.

I explained the courtroom procedure, described the judge, and how I would question him. I alerted him to some questions he might be asked on cross-examination. I also gave Jesse Ed a few tips about Schurtman's demeanor.

I told him that John and Yoko and Eddie would be in my office at 8:30 a.m.

"Meet us there," I said, "and we'll all drive to court together."

Chapter 25

John's Band's Farm Holiday

January 20, 1976
US District Court
New York City

JOHN AND YOKO WERE ON TIME ON TUESDAY morning as was Eddie. Jesse Ed was not. I waited a few minutes, then called his room. No answer. I kept trying. No answer. John was not happy.

"I knew it," he said. "Irresponsible musicians. You can't count on them. They're unreliable. I knew Jesse Ed could be a problem." *This is John Lennon, one of the great rock 'n' rollers, complaining about unreliable musicians. Has he blotted his so-called "lost weekend" from his memory?*

I continued calling Jesse Ed's room to no avail.

"Let's go," I finally said. "Don't worry about him, John. I'll arrange to have someone find him and bring him to court."

John frowned, shrugged his shoulders, and got up. I led the group through the reception area when the elevator doors opened. Out bounced Jesse Ed. I say "bounced" because he walked on the balls of his feet. He looked fantastic in a long fur coat over a green vested suit with a green shirt and a black tie. His long jet black hair hung over his shoulders. I reached him first.

"I've been calling your room since 8:30," I said. "There was no answer."

"Oh man, I must have been in the shower," he said. "I just got in." *Wonderful*, I thought. *One of my star witnesses has been out all night with Ronnie Wood doing who knows what.* I could only hope the unusual musicians' hours he seemed to keep regularly would not cause problems on the witness stand.

He, John, and Eddie greeted each other warmly with hugs and laughs. I didn't tell John that Jesse Ed had been out all night. We went downstairs, got into the limo, and headed downtown. The laughs and jokes continued during our ride. As we walked up the courthouse steps, I reminded John about answering the judge's questions.

"Let him take you where he wants to go," I said.

"I will," replied John. "I'm ready for whatever he asks."

We were about to introduce our three most important witnesses to Judge Griesa. They would be his formal introduction to rock 'n' roll.

I called Eddie first. Six feet tall with sandy hair, he looked a little tense but loosened up when I began questioning him. He testified that he had been a musician, record producer, and recording artist for ten years. He played acoustic guitar on *Walls and Bridges* and *Rock 'n' Roll*.

He explained the difference between 7-1/2 and 15 ips tapes, stating that "the hiss level is outstanding in a 7-1/2 tape [and it is] primarily used for reference [to listen to] purposes . . . [i]n other words, it is just a copy."

When I asked him "to tell the Court what a lacquer master is," he testified:

"A lacquer master is made from the 15 inch tape and then is sent off to the factory, where they make what they call mothers, the metal parts that are then turned into stampers to make the record."

Judge Griesa, obviously interested and taking notes, interrupted.

        THE COURT: A lacquer master is made
    from the tape, right?
        THE WITNESS: Right.

THE COURT: And then you use the lacquer master to make a mother.

THE WITNESS: Right.

THE COURT: And a mother is --

THE WITNESS: It is the metal part.
The lacquer is a piece of plastic and
they make metal parts from that.

THE COURT: When you say 'metal part',
what is it?

THE WITNESS: It is a record made out
of metal.

THE COURT: All right, go ahead.

Eddie testified that May called him about playing on the
Rock 'n' Roll album a couple of weeks before he came to New
York from his home in New Hampshire. He, John, and May
drove up to Morris Levy's farm in Morris's Cadillac.

A crucial part of Eddie's testimony was that he didn't hear
any discussions in Levy's car or at any time that weekend about
John "doing an album for Morris Levy." John never told him
that "over the weekend or at any time thereafter."

I asked Eddie if he'd had any discussion with John during
the weekend about how the album was going to be marketed.

"Yes," he answered. "He [John] said to me—we were sitting on the couch together when we first arrived at the farm.
He said to me, 'I'm going to try to sell this album through the
media, but I don't think the record company will go for it.'"

As to the actual recording sessions the week of October 21,
Eddie testified that neither Morris Levy nor Phil Kahl were
present at Record Plant when they were recording.

On cross-examination by Schurtman, Eddie testified that
he knew nothing about the case and had never discussed it
with John Lennon, May Pang, or Harold Seider, adding, as to
Seider, "I don't even know who that is."

When Schurtman asked Eddie if the musicians used sheet
music or lead sheets when they rehearsed at the farm, he an-

swered, "No."

Schurtman had not taken the depositions of any of the musicians and had no idea how Eddie would respond to any of his questions. A cardinal rule of cross-examination is to never ask a question if you don't already know the answer.

He violated that rule during his cross-examination of Eddie (and Jesse Ed and John), and his follow-up questions elicited answers very helpful to our case.

> **Q** How did you know what the tunes were?
>
> **A** They were all old songs from the '50s that everybody knew, all the musicians knew the songs from the time they were children.
>
> **Q** Who suggested which songs should be rehearsed?
>
> **A** John did.
>
> **Q** In other words, John would start a song and everybody would join in?
>
> **A** Yes.

Excellent testimony for us. One of Levy's factual contentions was that supplying sheet music and lead sheets for the farm "rehearsals" was part of his "deal" with John. But Eddie testified that they weren't used because they weren't needed.

Schurtman got nothing helpful to Levy's case from Eddie, who was finally excused.

I then called Jesse Ed, who looked relaxed in his green suit. Judge Griesa stared at him. Jesse Ed testified he had been a professional musician for sixteen years, playing with Taj Mahal and the Faces. In addition to playing with John, he'd also played and/or recorded with Helen Reddy, Cher, Harry Nilsson, and Ringo Starr.

"Do you want some more?" he asked me.

"That's enough," I said. "Thank you."

He went on to testify that he'd met John in December 1968 at the filming of the Rolling Stones movie, *Rock and Roll Circus*, directed by Michael Lindsay-Hogg, in London, England. This was a concert headlined by the Stones featuring Jethro Tull, The Who, Taj Mahal, John Lennon, Yoko Ono, Marianne Faithfull, and a one-time only super group called The Dirty Mac, formed by John Lennon. The Dirty Mac comprised Keith Richards on bass, Eric Clapton on guitar, Mitch Mitchell of The Jimi Hendrix Experience on drums, and John Lennon on guitar and vocals. I was confident Judge Griesa knew none of these performers.

Jesse Ed said he worked with John on the Spector sessions in Los Angeles "around November of '73, I think." He also worked with John "[i]n the summer of '74 for the *Walls and Bridges* album."

He testified that May Pang made arrangements for him to come to New York. He didn't know who Morris Levy was. Klaus Voormann and his wife, Cynthia, flew to New York with him.

    Q And you were met at the airport by a limousine?

He corrected me:

    A By the driver of a limousine.

Judge Griesa got involved:

    THE COURT: You were met at the airport and driven right up to the farm, right, or did you stop in New York or what happened?
    THE WITNESS: We stopped at a liquor store.
    THE COURT: But you didn't stop at a

```
hotel in New York and lay over or any-
thing like that?
    THE WITNESS: No.
    THE COURT: You went more or less di-
rectly to the farm right?
    THE WITNESS: Yes, more or less.
```

After testifying that he, Klaus, and Cynthia had arrived at the farm at 2 a.m. Friday, Jesse Ed said he met Morris "Friday morning when I woke up."

```
Q  Was that at breakfast?
A  No, that was at lunch.
```

Jesse Ed testified he had no discussions with John, Morris Levy, May, or anyone else, including the other musicians, about John doing an album for Levy. When I asked if there were discussions about how the album would be marketed, he testified:

```
A  I had a discussion with May Pang
that the album was — they were trying to
set up the thing where they could sell
it as a TV mail order album, but that
there was some concern over John's re-
cord contract not allowing him to do
that.
```

I asked him if Morris Levy or Phil Kahl was at the October Record Plant recording sessions and he answered:

```
A  Nobody gets in John's sessions.
```

I ended my direct examination. Schurtman began his cross-examination. His initial questions were about the 1973 Spector sessions. Jesse Ed testified about the next time he heard about those recordings:

> **A** I think it must have been during the *Walls and Bridges* session. There was some talk, some small talk about trying to finish those up, there wasn't enough tunes to do a complete album and sometime we will have to get to work and finish that, record enough tunes to complete that album.
>
> **Q** With whom did you have that small talk?
>
> **A** John Lennon.
>
> **Q** Can you tell us as best you can recall, what John Lennon said about the Spector songs?
>
> **A** I think he said that some of them were crap and that you couldn't use them.

Schurtman's questions were not designed to elicit any information helpful to Levy's case. For example:

> **Q** When you were told that the rehearsal was going to be at a farm, did you express any surprise?
>
> **A** No, John never surprises me.

Jesse Ed remembered the titles of only a few songs rehearsed at the farm. When he was asked if they used "any sheet music" he answered:

> **A** I think there was a few lead sheets laying around, but you don't need a lead sheet to play "Tutti Frutti," you know.

I quickly glanced back at John. I didn't know what he thought of Eddie and Jesse Ed's testimony but I thought it was terrific.

When Schurtman got around to whether there was any talk during the weekend about who John Lennon was doing the album for, or how it would be marketed, he floundered again. Jesse Ed said there "was just a lot of polite chatter" during the rehearsals or meals and no talk about music, adding that "[w]e just had a good time, lots of laughs, you know."

He testified he was familiar with the manufacture of records, the pressing process and the difference between 7-1/2 and 15 ips tapes. When prodded, he said:

> **A** . . . I think engineering standards seem to agree that 15 inch per second gives you better quality sound . . .
> [s]ome people say 30 inch per second . . .
> In recent times . . . I don't know of any [instances where 7-1/2 inch per second tapes have been used].

During a discussion among Judge Griesa, Schurtman, and me about Schurtman's wanting to play a cassette of the Los Angeles Spector tapes—a cassette given by John to Morris at some unknown point in 1974—Jesse Ed, without being asked, volunteered brilliantly:

> THE WITNESS: Excuse me a second. I think maybe some of the original recordings might be able to be improved greatly and were those original recordings issued on a record they might be artistically embarrassing.

Thank you, Jesse Ed.

That ended his testimony. As he walked by me, I said, "Stick around. We'll have lunch."

"Cool, man," he replied.

Our first two witnesses set the stage for the testimony of our key witness, John.

Chapter 26

"How We Learned the Trade"

January 20, 1976
US District Court
New York City

IN THE WEEK BEFORE JOHN TESTIFIED, I outlined the areas I'd question him about so he could educate Judge Griesa about The Beatles and John Lennon. John and I reviewed the outline over the weekend of January 17 at the Dakota. After we finished, I knew he'd be able to explain his recording process to the judge.

On the witness stand John wore a plaid shirt, his butterfly/

BOB GRUEN

From the left, Judge Thomas P. Griesa; John, testifying; William Schurtman; and Jay Bergen, January 20, 1976.

spider tie, and a dark blue sport jacket. He identified himself, Ringo Starr, Paul McCartney, and George Harrison as the four members of The Beatles.

> **Q** When did The Beatles begin record-
> ing together approximately?
> **A** Well, I mean we made records be-
> fore in Germany, but officially our ca-
> reer started in 1962.

As for their EMI recording contract as individual artists and a group:

> **THE WITNESS:** As far as I under-
> stand, they own everything I do even if
> I speak.

John did not "have ... a clue" as to "how many record albums The Beatles distributed through EMI." He stated that he had "co-produced and ... produced" his own record albums and those of other artists, naming Harry Nilsson, Yoko Ono, David Peel, and Elephant's Memory.

The best way to explain John's fascinating testimony is to read the actual transcript pages.

> **Q** Mr. Lennon, can you describe the
> development of The Beatles and you as
> a recording artist, in other words, how
> The Beatles developed?
> **A** How we learned the trade?
> **Q** Yes.
> **A** Well, when you are 22 and you get
> your contract, you are so thrilled to be
> allowed in the studio and also you [are]
> ignorant, usually, that you have no idea
> what is going on, you just know you are

a live band and you have been playing in dance halls and somebody is going to put you on tape, record you and make a record, and over the years we learned how to make a record ourselves and how in some instances to improve it. We just learned the trade of recording over a few years until finally by about the third or fourth album we virtually had taken complete control of the recording, meaning we then knew what could and could not be done. So we had the last words on it, even though we still had a producer, we [oversaw] the recording session, and gradually over the years we learned everything about it, until we made all the decisions, including the cover of the album, what was written on it, just everything to do with the production and even the selling and the ads in the papers -- we controlled everything artistic about the albums.

Q When you say everything artistic about the album, you mean right from the selection of the songs up to how the record [is] going to be sold?

A Well, that we controlled virtually from the beginning, although it was pretty hard when you are very new at it, because they try and impose other people's songs on you, which is what happened at the very beginning of our contract, and we made a half-hearted effort to record another person's song. But we stood our ground and finally forced them to let us do our own songs, even though we really did not have that much power then.

So what I am saying, we were arrogant enough, if that is the right word, to want to record our own material when most people would have been thankful just to be in the studio.

Q Now, you mentioned the album cover.

A Yes.

Q Do you mean that The Beatles after the first few albums had total control over what the album cover was, the jacket?

A At first EMI would just decide. They even provided the photographer and told us where to stand, and they took the picture and they put it out. And they did that for the first few. I don't know. Maybe about the third album we got control of the cover.

•   •   •

THE WITNESS: Yes, I mean they were not obliged to let us control our own covers. As far as I know, I don't think it was written in the contract. I don't think people cared about it in those days. It was not normal for artists to do their own covers.

Q Were The Beatles one of the first groups to gain control of doing the covers and supervise that in total?

A I can only speak for pop music. I have a suspicion that jazz people and classical people have more control than did those of pop music. In general, nobody cared about their covers. Maybe they just put a picture of the artist on the front.

I then questioned John about how he produced records.

Q Now, would you generally describe the recording processes for the Court from the moment you got into the studio?

A Well, it varied from artist to artist.

Q In [your] experience tell us what procedures you followed?

A In general I take the group into the studio and in general I record my own songs, so I have to teach them the songs, either in the studio or outside of the studio. Generally I teach them inside the studio, like a rehearsal or run through.

And for that we would put it on just a one track or a two track. We would not waste time setting a 16 track machine, which cost money for the tape and it is not worth it. So we just run a rehearsal on a smaller tape. And then we will try after we run through all the songs and I have decided which ones they seem to be getting the best, after two days of that, say, I will start laying down the basic tracks for the first song. It usually take[s] the engineers an evening or half an evening to get the sound of the drums, then the sound of the bas[s], then the sound of the guitar, then the sound of the piano, and then a combin-

ation of all those people playing at
once.

Q You mean to get it at the right
level?

A The engineer has to know virtually what the drum is going to do, what
it is going to sound like when it is
hit, whether it is going to distort, so
that there has to be an interruption and
a sound check without having anything
to do with the song, then rehearse the
sound without me. The engineer will say
drummer, drum, play your tom-tom, and
he will play the tom-tom and adjust the
mikes and move them around and play the
tambourine or cymbals. They have to go
through the whole thing before they even
start the session.

Usually, I hire the studio, so I
know I am going to be there for a month;
I am usually there for ten days with
the musicians, and so all the instruments are set up already, but even with
that, after the run-through and the
sound check still each night they will
run through the sound of the instruments
again, because people come in and move
microphones, or the musicians forget and
they kick the amplifiers or they change
the volume.

Q You mean then before you start the
sessions?

A Yes, every night. That is why we
get there early and I generally like to
sing with the musicians. I may be in a
booth that is supposed to be soundproof.

But I like to sing with the musicians, because then I get the rhythm; I like to do it by feel. Quite often I can't use my vocal, but at least I know how it was.

THE COURT: When you say you can't use the vocal?

THE WITNESS: I can't use [it], sometimes it is no good, and I like to play an instrument myself. So if I am lucky, I get a vocal. But even though I am singing, I have to be listening to the drummer and the bass player and all. I go around and say, "Has anybody got any secrets I didn't hear?" Sometimes they [tell] you when it is too late, "Oh, yes, I played a wrong note here."

"Why didn't you tell me? I didn't hear it."

So it is a matter, I have to produce it listening hard and do this for ten days usually. I usually put ten tracks on an album. I will tell you the reason if you want to know.

Q   Yes.

A   In general, I put ten tracks because I have learned over the years -- well, everybody knows this -- after you get past 20 minutes the volume of a record has to go down, and it has something to do with the grooves getting thinner. I have had records over 20 minutes, but when it gets over 20 minutes, the volume goes down, and if you average out ten songs it works out to about 20 minutes a side. So it usually takes about ten days to play the basic tracks down with the musicians, and then usually I send them home, and if I am going to overdub, like a saxophone or xylophone or flute or whatever, I want to put it on, then I will hire a new lot of people with those instruments.

Q Talking about how long a record should be, what you mean is that there is just so much space on each [side] of a record for the sound that is going to be of a proper quality?

A Well, it is a matter of taste. I am not saying you [cannot] have more.

Q I am talking about what you do.

A [It can] be done to 28 minutes, but I don't like to do that, because I want the record loud, and if the groove is deeper you can get more bass drum, and it even goes to the selection of what to put nearest to the center of the record, because the nearer to the center of the record you get the quieter it has to be. The grooves change when you get to the middle. That is what I have learned from the engineers.

Q You say you like the records loud?

A Yes, I like them to have depth.

Q If you put your record on at a certain sound, say my stereo at home, it will play [at] a certain level, if you put on another record without adjusting the volume it may not be as loud?

A That is quite possible, yes.

Q Now, you started talking about the next step after you finish the first basic tracks with the musicians. What is next?

A Every time I go in I relearn the whole business. So sitting here cold it is hard to remember what I do next. Probably I take those things home, play them on a cassette, listen to them, and decide what kind of instrumentation I want to put over the top of it.

Q You mean what instruments in addition to the basic instruments that have been put on by you during these ten days?

A There is a chance that I have a few things I want to do with the tracks. In the meantime, I take them home and listen, or go to the studio and listen, and then decide the next phase, whether I am going to put in a rhythm section or something else.

Q Tell the Court how that is done.

A In general, you still record onto the 16 track, if you have not used up all the space. If you have used up all the space, which sometimes happens, as I also like to record with a percussionist [live] with me, then I will have to mix down a couple of tracks to make room for the strings and the saxophones, and if it is strings, they bring in a 30-piece orchestra or whatever I have ordered, and usually I have worked with an arranger or a writer, and I hum to him, and I want the cellist to go this way, I want the top violins to play this melody or counter-melody, and he will write it down for me, and then they will print it out so the ones that have to read the music, which is generally the violinists, can read what I want and record them.

Q And those additional instruments laid down on whatever tracks you have left?

A Yes, and if there are not any tracks, I will make tracks. Maybe I will wipe off the percussionist and come back another day. Maybe he is not necessary. Quite often I will wipe off my own guitar and make room for other instruments, or I will play the two instruments together.

.   .   .

BY MR. BERGEN:

Q Now, after you get these basic tracks down of the various instruments that you have just described, then you go in with additional instruments and lay those instruments down on the tracks?

A Yes.

Q You are the one who decides what additional instruments you will put down on these additional tracks?

A If it is my session.

Q If it is your session?

A Yes, if I am visiting somebody else, it is their prerogative, but on my sessions I choose everything.

Q Now, what happens next after you have laid down the additional tracks that you feel you want on the record?

A What happens then?

Q Yes.

A Well, then I have to go to the studio with the engineer and we have to try and make sense out of all the 16 tracks with all these different people playing, and the idea is to reduce the 16 tracks down to two tracks to make a stereo record, and that is called re-mixing, and that can take as much time as the recording. It is called remixing, and it is to reduce the 16 tracks down to two tracks.

Q Your two track left and right stereo?

A Yes.

Q What is the next step after you have mixed it down to the two tracks? What happens next?

A Then you listen to it and see what you have got. One of the problems or responsibilities of the engineer, more than the producer, although I have to remind him at times, is to make sure that the different sessions are compatible, meaning, on a Monday night if they record at one level -- it is up to the engineer what level they take it down -- on Tuesday night if he forgets to match it, when you come to the re-mix, there may be one track that is ten times louder than the other for no reason, because nobody touched their knob when you mixed them. If it is all done around the same period it will all sound pretty much the same, but if you do it at different DBs, different decibels, you have to see that it is done properly. And when you get into the master room, you can alter the whole record again in the master room, which I have done on a few records. It is just like virtually remixing the whole thing.

Q Going back to the re-mixing, you worked with and supervised the work of the engineer on the re-mixing?

A Sure, the engineer, to give you an analogy, is like the cameraman on a film, and I would be similar to the director, and so worked hand in glove with him all the time, and neither one conflicts with the other, and we rely on each other. I rely on him to tell me if he got the film, if the sunlight was all right, and he relies on me to say yea or nay, what I want or don't want.

Court recessed then for lunch. As soon as we all settled into the limo, I laughed.

"What are you laughing at?" John asked.

"Jesse Ed saying, 'You don't need a lead sheet to play "Tutti Frutti," you know.'" By that time we all were laughing.

"Or how about Eddie's line?" I added. "'We didn't use lead sheets because they were all old songs from the '50s that everybody knew. All the musicians knew the songs from the time they were children.'"

The laughter grew louder as we drove toward Sloppy Louie's.

"That was great, really great," John said. "You were both terrific, weren't they, Yoko?"

"Yes, they were," replied Yoko.

Eddie and Jesse Ed were glad their testimony was over and that it had gone well. Once at the restaurant, we sat at our usual table.

"Have you noticed that sometimes it's hard to hear Schurtman because he speaks with his mouth almost closed?" I asked John. "Like his teeth are clenched and he's talking through them."

Trying to imitate Schurtman, I clenched my teeth and said, "'Objection, Your Honor.'"

"Yes, that's it," John said. "The judge sometimes says, 'I can't hear you, Mr. Schurtman.' He does speak like that."

John tried his own imitation of Schurtman several times.

"Objection, Your Honor," he repeated, teeth clenched.

Laughter erupted at our table. This routine became a running gag throughout the trial. John imitated Schurtman in the limo or at lunch. Or I would state during testimony, "I can't hear you, Mr. Schurtman," and then glance back at John.

During lunch we reviewed the morning. Our two witnesses were very interested in John's testimony about the development of The Beatles and his recording process.

"Jay and I spent a lot of time outlining and reviewing how that happened," John said. "I felt very comfortable answering those questions. I got into a good rhythm right away. Thanks, Jay."

"You're welcome and thank you for putting in the time," I replied. "I loved it when Schurtman tried to interrupt the flow of your testimony and the judge brushed him off. And later Judge Griesa asked you questions. He wants to understand how the whole recording process works. And that's going to help us when you begin explaining why *Roots* is shoddy and cheesy."

On the way back to court, John instructed the driver.

"Please take Eddie and Jesse Ed wherever they want to go," he said. "You can pick us up around 4:30."

When we arrived at the courthouse I thanked Eddie and Jesse Ed for their great testimony, as did John and Yoko.

Chapter 27

John's Creative Process

January 20, 1976
US District Court
New York City

WHEN COURT RESUMED AT 2:15 P.M., I continued questioning
John about his recording process. Judge Griesa often interrupted. We were delighted when he did.

> **Q** Going back to the recording pro-
> cess, is it your practice between the
> recording of the initial tracks and the
> over-dubbing of other instruments to
> take some kind of a break between the
> two?
>
> **A** Generally between the basic tracks
> [before] I put in violins or saxophones,
> I take maybe a week or so or less to de-
> cide what to put on and also to arrange
> it with the arranger, meaning a guy that
> can write the music for me, and between
> the re-mixes and the masters I also usu-
> ally take a break because by then I have
> heard them so many times I can hardly
> hear them, I have to take a break before
> mastering.
>
> **Q** After you have completed the re-
> mixing and you take this break, what is

the next step in the recording process?

A Well --

THE COURT: May I interrupt you? I am probably not using the right technical terms, but you have testified about the initial recording.

THE WITNESS: Yes.

THE COURT: You told us about that this morning. And then you said at some subsequent point you might add instruments?

THE WITNESS: Yes.

THE COURT: And you might do that by adjusting and so forth, whatever is necessary to reduce the 16 tracks to the two track stereo?

THE WITNESS: That is a major operation. It is almost as important as the recording itself.

THE COURT: Now, I am a little uncertain. The break that you mentioned, is that between the initial recording and whatever instruments are to be added?

THE WITNESS: Because I have to decide what I am going to do, whether it is going to be saxophones, [violins], or whatever, and then I got to get a guy to write music and I have to tell him what I want. I not only want to think what I will want, but to decide what they play, and then I have to have the guy write it for me, and then I will go in.

THE COURT: After you have made that decision and the person has written the music, then you bring the other instruments in and you do your additional recording?

THE WITNESS: Yes.

THE COURT: Then after that you are ready to do the --

THE WITNESS: Mix down.

THE COURT: Mix down.

THE WITNESS: Or the re-mix, yes.

•   •   •

I picked up the questioning.

Q   What is the next process, the next step after the remixing?

A   After the remixing? Presuming you are still happy with it ten days later or whenever you come back to listen to it, you take it upstairs, or wherever the place is, to cut the master.

Now, generally, I have the mastering guy take a listen to it while I am away or while I am not listening to it just to see if there are any big problems, like did we put too much on and it will not make a record.

I don't know how to explain it. I know that sometimes you can put too much noise on a tape and it sounds all right to your ears, but the machine just won't take it. It happens rarely, but the guy will usually confirm it's all right, the stuff will cut okay.

Q   The master --

A   Then we go upstairs and make a master lacquer out of it.

Q   The mastering engineer is somebody

separate from the engineer who you work in the studio with on the remixing?

A What generally happens is about the night before or a day before you master it you take the 15 inch tape that we will call the master for now and you run it through any comments the engineers have from the mastering room, like maybe this one won't cut or this one is down a DB. Then you have to run it through an EQ master, which means equalized master, meaning you equalize all the tracks to make each track compatible with the other track.

Q Equalize the sound?

A Yes, of all the tracks. It's like you have to put it through a filter to make everything sound pretty much the same.

The judge began a long discussion about the *Rock 'n' Roll* recording process. John explained it was particularly difficult because the recordings from the Spector sessions, which had twenty-eight musicians playing, and his New York sessions, which had eight, had to be equalized.

After a discussion on equalization, I questioned John, who definitively said that a lacquer master is only made from a 15 ips tape—never from a 7-1/2 ips tape, adding that the latter are only used for reference or demos.

John outlined all that an engineer must do to a 15 ips tape in the mastering room: he goes track by track, tinkering, perfecting, putting more bass here, a little less treble there. In the mastering room, John added, timing is taken care of, too, as well as the sequencing of the songs, and if applicable, the fade-out.

BY MR. BERGEN:

Q The sequencing of the tracks on the record.

A Yes.

Q Is that important?

A That is as important as -- well, it is a very important process, because one tune can ruin another. Sometimes you can have a nice track that sounds good, but if you put it behind something -- well, simply, if you have two slow songs, sometimes it gets boring.

So a basic sort of rule of the game is if you have a fast one put a slow one. That's a simple way of putting it.

But there are lots of subtle differences. Maybe the horns -- putting them in order is like putting a show in order, a Broadway show.

Here Schurtman interrupted my questions and John's answers.

MR. SCHURTMAN: Your Honor, can I request --

A You have to build up -- you have to hold the listener for 20 minutes a side so he doesn't turn the record off. It is very important which song follows which song.

THE COURT: All right, Mr. Schurtman.

MR. SCHURTMAN: Your Honor, can I request that the witness define what he means by track in this instance.

THE COURT: I can't hear you.

MR. SCHURTMAN: Can I request the witness define what he means by track in this context, because I think he is now using track in a different sense.

THE COURT: All right.

Are you using --

THE WITNESS: Track, I mean each cut, meaning each song on the album.

THE COURT: So track sometimes means a song and track sometimes means a track, right.

THE WITNESS: Yes, yes.

Q When you talk about the order you are talking about the order of the songs in the album?

A Yes. I mean, it is one of the most painful processes, because sometimes you think you have a great track or song and then you put it next to something and it sounds disgusting and you have to go through the whole process again of maneuv[e]ring.

It is like a ji[g]saw puzzle, only there is no set answer, only you know the answer. So you can put the puzzle together and it seems to fit, but when you look at it it is wrong, so you have to pull it all apart again and do it again.

THE COURT: Maybe I misunderstood. You said a few minutes ago that the engineer making the lacquer master does it track by track.

THE WITNESS: Yes.

THE COURT: There did you mean song by song or did you mean track by --

THE WITNESS: Song by song.

THE COURT: Song by song, because by that time what he has is the two track tape anyway, he hasn't got the 16 tracks?

THE WITNESS: Oh, no. 16 tracks are forgotten about now. You don't hear about that again, unless somebody damages the master.

I resumed my questioning.

Q While the engineer is working on these different songs or tracks in the cutting room, do you work with him and supervise his work?

A Sure, I am there.

Q When you say "you," when you are referring to you, that the order of the tracks or songs may not sound right, you mean you as the artist whose record it is?

A Yes, or the producer.

Now, some people -- you know, some artists are just produced by people and they never know what is going on, you know. I mean, they just go in and sing and they go away.

But I produce my own records too, so I play two roles.

John went on to outline his role as producer: he takes home the rough lacquer master and listens to it on a normal speaker. Next comes the white label, or test pressing (the first time the album is put onto plastic "like a real album that you can bend"), which John gets to approve. If the white label is okay, the actual pressing of the records is the next step. EMI usually allowed John to make and approve all the lacquer masters for the US, the UK, Europe, and Japan.

At this point John and I had decided that his testimony would turn to the factual history of how Levy became "connected" to John through the "Come Together" settlement agreement.

Chapter 28

John's Truths Negate Levy's Lies

January 20, 1976
US District Court
New York City

We began with John testifying that in October 1973 he was working with Phil Spector on an album of "oldies but goldies," which he defined as "old rock and roll records" popular in the 1950s "[g]enerally, and early sixties." I asked him whether Phil Spector was a producer "[o]f popular records," meaning "pop" records.

"Some were popular," John replied. Touché.

John denied that "Come Together" was copied from "You Can't Catch Me." He described how a call about the "Come Together" case had interrupted the Spector sessions.

    A   It was about the third or fourth day of the Spector sessions and they were going rather well and somebody called me -- I don't know who -- and said, "the Come Together lawsuit is on in New York, you know, you are supposed to come."

    I said, "Don't do that. You know I am in the middle of working. You know I don't do anything other than work when I am working. I can't think about something else that happened years ago. Just

```
go and make a deal, leave me alone you
know.
```

John told Judge Griesa how the case was settled though the judge already knew that. He'd been the presiding judge before whom the settlement was entered on the court record in October 1973. John also related the chronology of events perfectly: Spector took the tapes and disappeared. The tapes were returned in July 1974. *Walls and Bridges* was recorded and released. Work on the Spector master tapes began.

I then took John through the October 8 meeting with Morris Levy. He basically repeated his deposition testimony, stating, "All I was interested in was saying what I had to say about the tapes. I was very nervous, because I did not know the man. And I heard he was annoyed at me."

John recounted that when he mentioned the possibility of selling the oldies album on TV, Levy had said, "I am an expert at that . . . that is my business . . . [I] would like . . . to put out the album on TV." John repeated his reply, "That is cool with me as long as it is all right with the record company [EMI]."

He said his policy is to tune out and be polite whenever a discussion veers into figures or business talk.

"All I had to say is, 'I'm with EMI. You have to ask EMI,' " John testified. "I didn't have to say anything more or think about it any more . . . [o]nce I relieved myself of the apology, I just relaxed."

After denying that he told Levy that he "considered that the Spector package was dead material," I explored the point further with John.

```
    Q  Had The Beatles or you as artists
ever had what you referred to as dead
material?
    A  One thing The Beatles and me never
like, the idea of having a lot of mate-
rial that is crummy left in the vaults,
```

```
for when you die in an airplane crash,
which is what a lot of rock and roll
people do, then they release this mate-
rial and they put strange people play-
ing on it, which happens to such artists
as Buddy Holly. So we did not make it a
practice to put a lot of stuff on tape.
The Beatles may have two tracks that
were never released, and one of them is
from 1962, and I have one, and there is
the Spector tape, so now I have three
that they could release if I died, which
I would hate to have released.
```

John denied that he told Levy that they had a "deal." He also denied ever talking about having made a "deal," contradicting Levy's testimony.

Judge Griesa had heard enough.

```
    THE COURT:  It seems to me, Mr. Ber-
gen, Mr. Lennon has told us his memory
of the meeting . . . [l]et's move on.
```

As for Levy's invitation to his farm to "rehearse" before the October 21 recording sessions, John testified that he agreed to go but only after "a lot of discussion." When I asked him what the discussion was, he gave a great answer that revealed John's dilemma as a rock 'n' roll icon.

"Well, can I just say it in my own words?" he asked the judge.

```
    THE COURT:  Yes.
    THE WITNESS: When I meet people, even
my own lawyers, they want me to go to
dinner with them and they want me to
go to dinner with their wives and see
```

their children, and Morris [is] human, you know, he has got friends and kids. So he wanted me to go to his farm. I get these requests all the time, to go to people's places. If I said yes all the time, I would be somewhere else but my own house, and I refuse and refuse. The first time he asked me, I had a nice respect[able] reason not to go, which was I was going to spend some time with a contemporary, Mick Jagger, in Long Island.

The second time he asked me, I thought, well, I have another respectable reason for not going, and I said, "I got a lot of musicians coming in on Monday and I always rehearse with them over the weekend at the studio." I rehearse at the studios so engineers can get the feel of it and the musicians are more relaxed than they are in a hotel room. And they are so bored in the hotel. And after meeting with Jagger, I came back from that weekend, and he says, "Come next weekend."

I says, "I can't come; I am working."

He says, "You can work on the farm."

I said, "I can't work. I don't want my musicians going all over the farm, drinking and eating. They would think it is a holiday." They are like children; you have to herd them in. You can't let them loose. Then it is not their responsibility. They are to rehearse. He said, "They can rehearse there." . . .

And, anyway, I gave all the polite

excuses I had not to go up to the farm
without saying, "Look Morris, I don't
want to go to your farm. I am busy. Forget it." And so I finally said, "Yes."

Whatever I brought up as an excuse
not to, he would give me a reason why it
would be all right. So I finally says,
"Okay."

People often wouldn't allow him to be a person—not John
Lennon of The Beatles, just John Lennon.

John's recollection of the weekend was interesting.

For about two days we rehearsed. We
had breakfast, and then we would rehearse an hour or two, and then somebody
would yell "Lunch," which is another
thing that never happened in the studio.
People were called during the middle of
the session.

•   •   •

I don't remember saying much to any
of the guests. They were sort of staring
at me as I rehearsed [. . .] There were
children; there were a couple of gray-
haired men there; there seemed to be 20
people; some were staying there; some of
them were passing through. I was thinking about the album and being as polite
as I could under the circumstances. I
really was holding my breath so I could
get on with the job. I don't remember
small talk.

Another day in the life of John Lennon—people staring at him.

John made it clear to Judge Griesa that there was no discussion during the weekend about the oldies album. He did not tell anybody he was doing an album for Morris. Nor did he tell any of the musicians. As John testified, "[t]here would be no reason to tell the musicians anything."

John also explained his reasons for performing each song on the *Rock 'n' Roll* album.

> **Q** I show you Plaintiffs' Exhibit 35, which is the Rock and Roll album. Can you tell the Court whether you had any particular reasons for performing each one of the songs on the *Rock and Roll* album?
>
> **A** Yes, there is a pretty good reason for each one.
>
> **Q** Can you tell us, please?
>
> **A** "Be-Bop-A-Lula" was one of the first songs I ever learned, and I actually remember singing it the day I met Paul McCartney. I was singing at the church and McCartney was in the audience. "Stand By Me" was one of my big albums in the dance halls in Liverpool. That was [a] Benny [*sic*] King number. And the same goes for "Be-Bop-A-Lula." I knew these songs as a child.
>
> "Ready Teddy" was a sort of guitar type song written by Little Richard and recorded by him.
>
> "You Can't Catch Me" was the Morris Levy song but it was Chuck Berry, anyway, so that was good enough reason to do it.

"Ain't That A Shame" was the first rock and roll song I ever learned. My mother taught it to me on the banjo before I learned the guitar. Nobody else knows these reasons except me.

"Do You Want To Dance" we had at some jam sessions in the West Coast featuring numerous stars and not worth mentioning the names of.

I tried to get the Reggae version, which is a kind of rhythm, and so I thought I would try it myself.

"Sweet Little [Sixteen]," I have been singing that, which [is a] Chuck Berry number that was also an old time favorite of mine.

"S[l]ippin' & Slidin' " was the B side of Long Tall Sally, which is the first Little Richard song I ever heard and was also recorded by Buddy Holly, so that covers a little of both. It was a song I knew. It was easier to do songs that I knew than trying to learn something from scratch, even if I was interested in the songs.

"Peggy Sue," I have been doing that since [it] came out, and Buddy Holly did it, and, in fact, I used to sing every song that Buddy Holly put out.

"Bring It On Home To Me" is one of my [all time] favorite songs, and, in fact, I have been quoted as saying I wish I had written it, I love it that much, and I was glad to be able to do it.

"Send Me Some Lovin'" is a similar kind of song, and that was done originally by Little Richard, again one of my favorites, and also Buddy Holly.

"Bonie Maronie" was one of the very earliest songs, along with "Be-Bop-A-Lula," and I remember [sing]ing it the only time my mother saw me perform before she died. So I was hot on "Bonie Maronie." That is one of the reasons.

Also, I liked Larry Williams, who recorded it.

"Ya Ya" I did because it was Morris', and it was a good song. It is an easy song.

John also had a good reason to include "Just Because." He said Phil Spector talked him into it.

Chapter 29

John Finalizes *Rock 'n' Roll*—February 4-5, 1975

January 20, 1976
US District Court
New York City

JOHN THEN PROVIDED DETAILED TESTIMONY ABOUT THE TWO
7-1/2 ips reel-to-reel tapes he gave Levy on November 14,
1975. Levy knew John was in Record Plant October 21–25,
recording the rest of the album. He could not possibly have
"finished" and finalized the album for release in the twenty
days between October 25 and November 14.

John testified that Morris:

> [. . .] asked me a few times but I
> can't tell you when. He asked me quite
> a few times for tapes and I kept say-
> ing, you know, "They are not finished."
> I don't sort of like crummy tapes be-
> ing handed around. But when I finished, I
> gave them to him. I did enough work on
> them, so I was not embarrassed by lis-
> tening to them or having them outside
> the studio. . . .
> Well, I think I was in his club . . .
> he was asking me again, you know, and I
> virtually didn't have -- you know, what
> could I say. So I said, "What do you

> want, a cassette or a 7-1/2," and he
> said [something] about playing it in the
> office and giving him a 7-1/2.

Once again, instead of being rude and saying no, John gave in. He arranged with the Record Plant to have two 7-1/2 ips reel-to-reel-tapes made. Thom Panunzio, a young assistant engineer, delivered them to John at the Club. John testified that when he gave Levy the tapes, Levy did not tell him "that he was going to use it to put out an album." When I asked John if he intended that Levy use the tapes to put out an album, he replied, "I had no idea he was going to do that," shutting the door on the notion that John gave these tapes to Levy to make a record album.

Schurtman objected to John's answer.

"I will let it stand," Judge Griesa ruled. "I think it is pretty obvious. I mean, not obvious, but I think this is the purport of the witness' testimony." The judge knew from John's testimony that he'd sent an unfinished version of the *Rock 'n' Roll* album for Levy to listen to—not to make an album. But the judge really nailed down the point:

> THE COURT: . . . Did you say to Mr.
> Levy that he was authorized to use this
> tape to make a record album?
> THE WITNESS: No, because even a pi-
> rate record I would prefer him to have a
> good one.
> MR. SCHURTMAN: What was that?
> THE WITNESS: Even if it had been a
> pirate record, I would prefer them to
> have a 15 inch [per second] one that I
> approved.

In order to ensure that the judge understood John had not completed work on the album, I asked him what work he did after giving the two 7-1/2 ips tapes to Levy.

> THE WITNESS: Well, I had to equalize
> both recordings, like I tried to explain
> earlier, which is the West Coast and the
> East Coast recordings. I edited some of
> the Spector tapes down, because all of
> them were miles too long, so I cut out
> chunks of them. I finalized the version of
> "You Can't Catch Me," I finalized my ver-
> sion of "You Can't Catch Me" in the man-
> ner in which Phil Spector had rough mixed
> it the night we recorded it.

Schurtman raised a question about establishing dates as
to when John did this work in the studio. I agreed to stipulate
that the 7-1/2 ips tapes were given to Levy on November 14.

"All I am trying to find out is if the work he did afterwards
in fact came after the delivery of the tape," Schurtman said.

> THE WITNESS: Oh, yes. I can say that,
> yes because it is different.

Then Judge Griesa and John began another discussion
about the work John did on the album after November 14 and
his usual process in the studio.

The judge, being a musician, probed in more detail to make
sure the album was not finished when John gave the tapes
to Levy. John's descriptions of the two different versions of
"You Can't Catch Me" showed a major difference between the
inferior rough cut John gave Levy and the more finished final
version.

All during the creation of *Rock 'n' Roll*, John had planned to
apply Phil Spector's edit of "You Can't Catch Me" at the very
end of the process. The night the song was recorded in LA, he
said, Spector had made a "beautiful cut."

"He copied the intro to 'You Can't Catch Me,' which was very catchy, and he tape copied it," John explained. "In the middle of the song he cut it and the whole song began again. So we have this intro, a version, and then the intro again."

The change was done with bongos—just drums and voice, he added, calling the move "a brilliant piece of editing."

The 7-1/2 ips tape, which John gave Levy, did not include the edit. Since John made the change at the end, the maneuver was reflected in the 15 ips tape. The Spector edit was a significant change.

This began another judge/John colloquy in which John explained the final step in the recording process—making the lacquer master.

THE WITNESS: This when we had the final 15 inch thing, tape, and were trying to make the lacquer from it, and this is when I finally decided at the last minute, do I want to change the order of something, because it won't cut well, it still doesn't sound good, so we can change the order or drop the track. So that's when I did this.

THE COURT: And this is to make the absolute final 15 inch tape.

THE WITNESS: The final --

MR. BERGEN: No, the final lacquer master.

THE WITNESS: The final lacquer. . . . But the final artistic decision is made in that room then.

THE COURT: All right. That is in the process of making the lacquer master.

THE WITNESS: Yes, from the 15 inch tape.

·　·　·

    THE COURT: Then you end up with this
revised 15 inch tape?
    THE WITNESS: Yes.
    THE COURT: And it is from that you
start in and make the lacquer master?
    THE WITNESS: Yes.

The parties then stipulated that John's studio work was done on February 4 and 5, 1975, and that the lacquer master parts were cut on February 6 and shipped to Capitol.

The day ended before John could finish his testimony on this critical issue—what actual work he did on the album between November 14 and February 4 and 5, when he finished the album. We would pick up where we left off the next day.

On the way uptown, I asked John, "I saw Bob Gruen in court this afternoon. What was he doing here?"

"I had him come down to take a picture of me testifying," John replied.

"You know that's not really permitted," I said, smiling. "It may even be some kind of a violation of law."

"It's okay," John said. "He covered the camera with his coat."

"Why the picture?"

"Someday I'm going to write an album of songs about all my and The Beatles' legal problems," John said. "That picture is going to be the album cover."

One thing I'd learned to appreciate about John was that he often thought ahead.

Chapter 30

John's Fall 1974

January 21, 1976
US District Court
New York City

BEFORE JOHN RETOOK THE STAND, Howard and I discussed with him what happened after November 14. We explained that Judge Griesa wanted to know what work he had done and his usual practice once he completed the basic tracks and over-dubbing. He had given some testimony about the period after November 14, but the judge was interested in hearing more detail. John thought he'd be able to do that.

When I asked John whether he was working on the *Rock 'n' Roll* album after November 14, he said, "Well, I never stop working on the thing until it goes out. I mean, I work on it at home—." Schurtman objected, trying to prevent John from answering and claiming what he said was "repetition" of yesterday's testimony. The judge disagreed.

> THE COURT: I think that was some-
> thing that was left open at the close of
> yesterday's session.
>   MR. BERGEN: I think that is where we
> stopped.
>   THE COURT: Certainly it wasn't
> clear. We had the description of the
> recording, then we had the description
> of that work that was done on February 4

and 5, or about, and then we were going
to try to explore what may have happened
in between.

    MR. BERGEN: I think we kind of
jumped ahead to February.

    THE COURT: Fine.

Without needing to have my question repeated, John
immediately answered.

    A In those breaks I take in between
physically being in the record studio, I
have rather sophisticated equipment at
home, which I take sometimes 7-1/2's,
sometimes 15's, nearly always cassettes,
of whatever the current state of the album is, and I won't listen to it for a
few days, then I will stick it on either
a cassette or a large reel -- I have a
big Sony machine which is pretty professional --

        •   •   •

    A I did it on this album. In fact,
I have even had -- I can't be specific
as to which period, but I did have the
engineer, Jimmy Iovine, working in the
house once trying to make me an edit
because I couldn't wait until the next
time we get to the studio to see what
it's like.

    What I will do is I will play the
things and I will think about them.
Sometimes I will play it and just listen to the whole thing without making

any comment to anybody, but I am listening in my head, you know, maybe I can do this, maybe I can do that.

THE COURT: I am going to ask you this: At this time what we are talking about is the period November, December, January of '74-'75, right?

THE WITNESS: This is in between finishing the recording and the mixing and going into the cutting room.

THE COURT: Right.

THE WITNESS: That [period] is a period when I will be -- well, the only place I will probably listen to the stuff is at home, meaning listen to it on a cassette and decide if the order is correct. I know the details of the music, so I can just listen casually to it.

Maybe once a week I will listen just to see how I react to the music.

THE COURT: Were you working on any other projects at this time?

THE WITNESS: No, I only had this one thing to finish.

Q Can you tell us what you mean by you had this one -- I am sorry. I didn't hear your Honor's question.

You were talking about other projects?

A Yes. I mean, I might have had other songs in my head. I mean, it's hard to say when I stop work and when I don't. I mean, even sitting in this courtroom I might start thinking of music to write or some lyrics.

But basically I was working on that

album and even though I try and get away
from the stuff before the final push, the
final mastering of it, I can't help playing it every other day or so to see if
it inspires me or if I get the answer to
a problem I might have.

•   •   •

THE COURT: The question I would have,
Mr. Bergen, I am interested as I sit
here thinking about it, knowing what in
reasonable detail Mr. Lennon was doing
about this record [between November 14
and February 4.] And I am interested in
knowing, for instance, from his standpoint why there would be this length of
time required to complete the record.
Was he waiting for some decision on a
contract? Was he needing from an [artis-
tic] standpoint something to complete
the record? That is all necessary to
make this thing hang together for me. So
you may pursue that harder.

With prompting, John testified: "I had promised Elton
John that if a record I made with him ["Whatever Gets You
Thru the Night"] got to No. 1, I would appear on stage with
him, and it happened to get to No. 1. So I was obliged to go
on stage with him" on Thanksgiving night at Madison Square
Garden.

The judge asked John what he did on the *Rock 'n' Roll*
album "from an artistic standpoint" after the October 21 to 25
recording sessions and John recapped his earlier testimony.

THE COURT: I think I get the picture.

Elton John and John Lennon at Record Plant, Summer 1974.   BOB GRUEN

John then testified that he had "[o]ne long session of listening, play back" of the album in December at Record Plant just before Julian arrived from England.

He briefly described the Christmas holidays trip with Julian and May. There was no discussion of business with Levy or anyone else in Florida. He and Levy "had certain ground rules where if he tried to talk to me about business I just wouldn't answer and he wouldn't try me."

Harold Seider came to Florida to explain the complicated "Beatles-Apple settlement agreement" dissolving their partnership.

John and May spent two days at Disney World with Levy, his son, Adam, and Julian. Otherwise, John "spent a lot of the time indoors or keeping out of the sun, because "I'm not very, you know, good in the sun. It gets to me." They sat at a cabana by the pool but John "didn't spend a lot of time there because people kept coming around me, so I spent a lot of time in the room. And then at night—I was reading, as a matter of fact, in the bedroom most of the time."

Once again to stop Levy's guests "coming around" him,

John hid in the condo.

John had a problem remembering dates of specific events. When I asked him about a photograph he wanted to use for the album cover, he recalled one "taken of me in Hamburg around about 1961 by this German photographer, and it is a photograph of me just standing in a doorway when I'm about 21, and it was around about the period when I would have been singing" the oldies songs he recorded on *Rock 'n' Roll*.

"And the sequence, if you get mad at me again, I don't know the sequence, but around about some period there was a Beatles Festival . . . it turns out this photographer has moved from Germany and living in America . . . So not only did I have the original pictures he had given me in Germany, but we could get brand new ones, also."

I laughed to myself because I had no idea what John meant when he said, "if you get mad at me again."

On January 28 John met in New York with Al Coury, Capitol's vice president of A&R (artist repertoire) responsible for John and The Beatles, about marketing the oldies album. Also present were Roy Kohara and Dennis Kileen from Capitol's Art Department, May Pang, and Harold Seider.

Elton John and John Lennon at Record Plant, Summer 1974.   BOB GRUEN

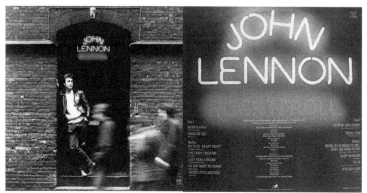

Rock 'n' Roll album cover front (left) and back.　　　　JüRGEN VOLLMER

John testified, "[t]his is the first time I had confronted them with the idea of how about let's put it on TV and I explained why I thought it might be a good idea." He was concerned about the critics lying in wait for the long-delayed album. Coury told him "it would be a lousy idea" because it would anger the usual marketers of John Lennon and Beatles records, the mom-and-pop stores, the large retail chains."

John realized "everybody would be furious at me."

The Capitol executives convinced him *Rock 'n' Roll* "will do alright" and presented a marketing campaign that John accepted. It included a mock-up of the album cover where someone had drawn in "*John Lennon Rock and Roll* . . . and they had written Rock and Roll in neon" lettering on the back of the cover. John liked it. "I said, 'Oh, great, that is the title, because that is what the whole album is about, it is just that, it is rock and roll. So we don't have to think of some extra title.'"

They acquired the right to use Jürgen Vollmer's 1961 black-and-white photo for the album cover that night.

The decision was made that Capitol would release *Rock 'n' Roll* through normal retail channels. The Morris Levy TV marketing idea was dead!

Court adjourned until the next day.

Chapter 31

A New Art Form: Album Covers

January 22, 1976
US District Court
New York City

WHEN THE TRIAL RESUMED JOHN TESTIFIED that the next thing he recalled was May telling him that Levy had called her. Levy told her that he was putting "the tapes out" and John could edit them if he wanted to. John was perplexed:

"I was shocked and I thought he had a nerve asking me to edit the tapes while he is going to put them out, anyway, but I was a bit stunned and scared because I thought I was in trouble. . . ."

Jimmy Iovine later called him at home and asked, "'Hey, what is going on? Your record is on TV.'" Jimmy told him it was on Channel 9. John finally saw the commercial the next day, Sunday, February 9.

Roots album cover.   *Roots back cover.*

John criticized the *Roots* cover from an artistic standpoint:

". . . I mean, this is nothing like anything I have produced myself. The picture is out of focus; it is an old picture of me. That does not matter. It's just a lousy looking cover, the colors, I don't like. I would not allow Capitol to advertise other artists' records on my cover. This is like endorsing whatever these other packages are. It is just not a good looking album."

This was the perfect time for John to explain the craftsmanship he and The Beatles took with their album covers. John and I had picked covers to introduce into evidence.

Our album cover court exhibits were CB-1, *This Is The Beatles*, 1964; CB-2, *Sgt. Pepper's Lonely Hearts Club Band*, 1967; CB-3, *Rubber Soul,* 1965; CB-4, and *Walls and Bridges*, 1974.

As The Beatles gained control of their album covers, they transformed them into an art form over time. They and John included foldouts, posters, and other presents in the package. As John testified, "It gets like Christmas." Sgt. Pepper's is a good example. It also added (for the first time) each song's lyrics on the back of the album jacket.

Judge Griesa was curious.

THE COURT: Why was the *John Lennon* [*Rock 'n' Roll*] so much less elaborate than, say, *Walls and Bridges*, which has the folding cover which has the little pamphlet inside?

Any reason for that?

THE WITNESS: Partly to do with time factor. But also that's why I was saying to Jay, perhaps they should show a margin cover which is pretty straight.

You don't always have a gimmick or a folder; you don't have to have something in it.

And Roy Kohara didn't come up with something like this, and there was no time.

I knew what the cover should look like but we hadn't decided on the inside.

Q When you say there wasn't any time, Mr. Lennon, can you explain what you mean by that?

A Because Capitol said we have got to go now, you know, and I just went in and cut the thing and sent it to them. There was no time for gimmicks or posters or anything.

THE COURT: Are you saying that you -- well, can you tell me whether or not you intended to have some, as you put it, gimmicks or posters or -- cut outs or something like that?

THE WITNESS: One of the ideas I had I was finally a version of it I used on the sheet music because I put the sheet music out myself with Lennon Music, and I worked with a guy on designing the book and we did a few little gimmicks that might -- I would have used in there only I didn't have time.

Q Mr. Lennon is this what you are talking about? (Handing).

MR. SCHURTMAN: May I just have a continuing objection so I don't have to keep getting up, to the witness state of mind, thoughts, stream of consciousness and so forth?

THE COURT: Overruled.

A This is the sheet music that we put out. And I had wrote a little piece.

THE COURT: Well, let's get that

marked.

 THE WITNESS: To explain --

 MR. BERGEN: Can we mark it? I will give it right back.

 (Plaintiffs' Exhibit CD for identification.)

 Q I am handing you Plaintiffs' Exhibit CD. (Handing.)

Exhibit CD was a sixty-four-page booklet John had prepared and designed in the form of a program for a live "show." It contained the sheet music for each song on *Rock 'n' Roll* with photos of the original performers of the songs. The cover features the same photo of John that appears on the album cover.

 MR. SCHURTMAN: May I see them?

 THE COURT: What?

 MR. SCHURTMAN: May I see them?

 THE COURT: Yes, certainly.

 MR. SCHURTMAN: Thank you. May I inquire as to the purpose for which these exhibits are offered?

 THE COURT: Mr. Bergen.

 MR. BERGEN: The purpose is to show what Mr. Lennon and the other Beatles and primarily Mr. Lennon, with respect to CD and CB4 [*Walls and Bridges*], what was their practice, normal practice with respect to album covers and how The Beatles and Mr. Lennon gradually took control of the entire production of an album and how, as Mr. Lennon has said, how important that is to him as an artist.

 THE COURT: And is there any objection?

 MR. SCHURTMAN: No objection.

 THE COURT: All right, received.

(Plaintiffs' Exhibits CB1 through 4 and
CD are received in evidence.)

When I asked John whether there were differences between *Roots* and *Rock 'n' Roll*, other than the quality of the
album covers, he spoke about the differences.

BY MR. BERGEN:

Q Mr. Lennon, other than what you
have testified to about the album cover
and the Roots album, are there any differences between the Roots album, Exhibit
34, and the Rock and Roll album, Exhibit
35? (Handing).

A Apart from engineering things,
like how they made the tape --

Q Are you referring to the 7-1/2?

A Yes. It's just a different album.
A, they have got two tracks on, which I
dropped and B, even if I had le[f]t them
on, they were different, my version of
"Be My Baby," which they left on is different.

Even up to the last minute, I was
still editing for two tracks, I finally
dropped.

Q What was the other track you finally dropped?

A "Angel Baby."

Q You were editing that up until the
last minute?

A My version of "Be My Baby" is different from their version, even if I left
it on the album. I cut it in half. It's
much better than this.

Griesa asked for a list of the songs on *Roots* and *Rock 'n'*

Roll. John emphasized the songs were in a different order on each album and that *Roots* ran twenty-two to twenty-three minutes per side, which negatively impacts sound quality, while *Rock 'n' Roll* ran twenty minutes.

> THE COURT: Now, this "You Can't Catch Me," did you say yesterday that that's different?
>
> THE WITNESS: Yes, that's very different. Because I have the original Spector's edit on my version.
>
> THE COURT: All right.
>
> BY MR. BERGEN:
>
> **Q** Are there any other differences you can think of, Mr. Lennon?
>
> **A** Well, you know, the quality must be different because this was made from a 7-1/2 and this was made from a 15, but I haven't heard it.
>
> THE COURT: Well you haven't listened. All right.
>
> THE WITNESS: But it's a fact of life.

Wrapping up, John spoke about how the *Roots* album damaged his artistic reputation.

> BY MR. BERGEN:
>
> **Q** Now, Mr. Lennon, do you believe that your reputation as an artist has been damaged in any way by the *Roots* album?
>
> MR. SCHURTMAN: Objection.
>
> **A** Yes.
>
> THE COURT: Yes, I will overrule that.
>
> **A** I think it's been [damaged] by the fact that the thing is out. And it looks

so bad and it didn't meet with my ap-
proval, and the public was confused as
to what was what. And which had my ap-
proval and which didn't and I just don't
think it does me any good at all to
have that cheap album going around with
tracks I don't like on it. With a lousy
picture out of focus, and it's almost
so ludicrous it's ridiculous. Even the
bootlegs on the market look better than
that.

John and I then went through a series of questions establishing key points: John had nothing to do with the production
or sale of *Roots*. He hadn't given anyone else, including Levy,
written or oral permission to use his name and likeness to distribute or sell *Roots*. And he'd never told Levy or the plaintiffs
they could sell *Roots* without EMI's permission.

These questions ended John's direct testimony. Since we
were taking witnesses out of order, Schurtman's cross-examination of John would not begin until later in the trial.

Chapter 32

May Pang and Yoko's Coat

January 26-28, 1976
US District Court
New York City

The direct and cross-examination of Phil Kahl, testifying on behalf of Big Seven and Adam VIII, ended in the late afternoon. I called May Pang, who'd been sitting in the courtroom all day.

May Pang was an important witness. She confirmed much of John's testimony (and Harold Seider's) about the October 8 meeting with Levy. I was almost finished with her direct testimony when we adjourned for the day.

As I was putting away my files, John whispered to me.

"Jay, you have to get May out of the courtroom and into the elevator," he said.

"What? What's the problem?" I asked.

"She's wearing Yoko's winter coat," he replied. "We can't be on the same elevator with her. You have to get her out of here."

"Yoko's coat?" I said. "I don't understand."

"Please," said John.

"Okay, I'll take care of it." May was talking to Howard. I walked over to them.

"Let's step outside into the hall so we can talk," I suggested. When we'd left the courtroom, I turned to May.

"You were terrific. Perfect," I said. "We'll start with you in the morning. Please get here about 10:30. Dress conservatively, as you did today. Schurtman will cross-examine you at some point. All you have to do is keep to the facts as you remember them. If you don't remember something, it's okay to say you don't remember. Thank you again for being so helpful, May."

"You're welcome," she said.

While speaking I slowly moved us closer to the elevators. Finally, one of them arrived. May got on. The doors closed. I never asked John what the problem was with May wearing Yoko's coat.

The next morning, January 27, May Pang arrived on time but she had poured herself into a form-fitting one-piece chamois dress. May was a beautiful young woman and she looked great, but we were in court. When I called her to the witness stand, Judge Griesa tried not to stare at her. He failed. Later in the morning Schurtman completed his cross-examination. May emerged from that unscathed.

I resumed my cross-examination of Levy before we broke for lunch. He kept dodging questions I asked about telephone conversations he'd had in January 1975 with Allen Klein. Levy had asked Klein who had the rights to sell John Lennon records through "retail fulfillment centers" and "foreign sales outside North America." These were critical issues in determining what Levy knew prior to releasing *Roots* and filing his two lawsuits.

To refresh Levy's recollection, I read him an excerpt from Allen Klein's deposition taken only months earlier.

From Allen Klein's deposition:
Q Did you [Mr. Klein] at any time ever tell Mr. Levy that if he had Mr. Lennon's permission he could sell and distribute the *Roots* album outside of North America without EMI permission?

A Absolutely not. In fact, I told him exactly to the contrary.

Q When did you tell him that?

A Oh, God. Probably January, January,

```
February, right after he informed me --
because he asked me to in effect reconfirm
that I had said to him that Apple Records,
Inc. in New York had the rights. I told him
my understanding, that they did, but that
it was only for the United States and maybe
Canada and certainly not for retail out-
lets, retail fulfillment centers.
```

I then asked Levy: "Does that refresh your recollection about a conversation you had with Mr. Klein?"

```
    MR. SCHURTMAN: Your honor, I don't
see any inconsistency.
    THE COURT: Does this refresh your
memory that he told you this in January
or February 1975?
    THE WITNESS: Yes.
    THE COURT: All right.
```

At this point, court recessed for lunch.

Levy's admission that Allen Klein had told him in January/February 1975 that he needed EMI's permission to sell the *Roots* album outside North America further undercut his original claims about the key provisions of the October 8 oral agreement.

Judge Griesa's "All right" would prove to be significant later in the afternoon.

When court resumed, Schurtman called Allen Klein to the stand. Klein testified until just before court adjourned for the day. Prettyman, Grumbach, and I each cross-examined him. When I questioned Klein he testified that John Lennon did not tell him he "was giving the [oldies] album to Morris Levy."

Judge Griesa interrupted my examination, eliciting significant testimony from Klein.

THE COURT: Are you saying that in one
of the conversations [with Levy in early
February 1975] at some point you specifically said that in your view Apple
[i.e., John Lennon] had no rights for
retail store sales and Apple [i.e., John
Lennon] had no rights for foreign sales?
THE WITNESS: Yes . . . I wanted
[Levy] to understand that there certainly was never any grant by EMI to Apple
of mail order rights which could be sold
through any retail outlet [like Kor-
vettes, Woolworth's].

Allen Klein was finally excused.

Judge Griesa, however, must have still had in mind Levy's
key admission just before the lunch recess to which he'd said
"All right." Klein had told Levy that Apple Records' rights were
"only for the United States and maybe Canada." He turned to
Schurtman and asked him a crucial question:

THE COURT: Look, Mr. Schurtman, I
want to be clear what you claim this
contract consisted of. We have gotten
- as we go farther we get more and more
information on the possible differentia-
tion between the status of US mail order rights, US retail store rights and
foreign rights of all kinds, and we have
the position more clearly outlined all
the time of EMI and Capitol.
Now, I know there are issues all the
way through and I am not trying to summarize it, but at this point I really
want to know what Mr. Levy or what the
plaintiffs claim was the contract which

was made. *What was it?* (emphasis added)

What followed were several evasions by Schurtman and admonishments by Judge Griesa, for example: "No, no. You tell me what the agreement was … Not what the discussion was; what the agreement was … Wait a minute … That isn't an agreement. That is a representation."

Finally, the judge laid down the law, so to speak.

> THE COURT: I am being very careful to ask you, was the agreement for Mr. Levy to distribute this through mail order, through retail fulfillment centers, US, Foreign, or what? What was the agreement?
>
> MR. SCHURTMAN: The agreement was that Mr. Levy's company would promote these records over television by mail order in the United States.
>
> It was also agreed that if *EMI consent could be obtained* they would also distribute it, Mr. Levy's company would distribute it, through retail fulfillment centers *and/or abroa*d. That was the agreement on that point. (emphasis added)

Schurtman added:

> The other terms of the agreement were that this would be a package for a *single television promotion*. The parties did not agree on any specific length of time. They simply said *one TV promotion*. (emphasis added)

These were *not* the provisions of the agreement which had been alleged repeatedly by Levy since January 1975.

Schurtman's admission was stunning.

The judge made a critical observation.

> THE COURT: Just a moment. Just a mo-
> ment.
>
> There are just lots of questions
> that come to mind. One is, Mr. Schurt-
> man, there is a serious question in my
> mind as to whether I could -- you know,
> it would be reasonable to find or assume
> that there would be this contract cov-
> ering mail order only, but leaving in
> abeyance, so to speak, the distribution
> through retail fulfillment centers.

Judge Griesa was pointedly challenging Schurtman's new version of the plaintiffs' claims. He specifically asked Schurtman for:

> [. . .] a list of references to all
> the testimony about the October 8th
> meeting and then I would like to get a
> list of references to all conversations,
> whether at the October 8th meeting or
> not, about this question of the rights,
> so to speak, the conversations about
> getting permission, calling Len Wood,
> going to England, who had the rights,
> giving rights, and so forth . . . [o]f
> all witnesses.
>
> MR. SCHURTMAN: We will do as much as
> we can.

(Schurtman never provided that list to Judge Griesa, stating the next morning, "I was not clear last night as to the form you wanted them in.")

MR. SCHURTMAN: Can I just finish what
I was saying before and leave you with
one last thought on the oral agreement.
THE COURT: Yes.
MR. SCHURTMAN: This is that when the
parties made the deal they did discuss
the fact, or they discussed it subse-
quently, that at some point it would be
put into writing. Nobody ever contem-
plated that this would be an oral agreement for all times. . . .

The judge then permitted me to speak.

MR. BERGEN: Your Honor, this is the
first time the defendants have heard
since this case started a year ago that
the alleged contract, the alleged oral
contract, was one for mail order rights
in the United States and then EMI's
permission would be obtained when they
would go on to something else.
It is also the first time that the
defendants have been told that this was
a package for a single TV promotion and
that the parties did not agree to any
specific period of time.

I then read the paragraph of the federal complaint entitled
"The October 1974 Agreement," which set forth the alleged
"worldwide" agreement. At Judge Griesa's request, he was
handed Levy's January 9 letter.
I added that the plaintiffs and Levy had repeated the same
language "[e]very time we have asked them what the agreement was."
Finally, I rebutted Schurtman's false statement that "at

some point [the deal] would be put into writing."

I read from Levy's deposition:

> **Q** At the conclusion of that meeting
> did you anticipate that the deal which
> you felt you had reached would be re-
> duced to writing at a subsequent date?
> **A** Not really, no.

Judge Griesa then asked the defendants to provide him with copies of every document filed by Levy and the plaintiffs where they had asserted the worldwide agreement. As he adjourned court for the day, the judge added that he wanted to promptly "come to grips with this question of whether there was an agreement or not."

> THE COURT: I will hear all the evi-
> dence that is necessary on both sides on
> that point, but I want to -- I think we
> are zeroing in on that and I think we
> can continue and get some resolution of
> this problem.

Court then adjourned to 10:00 a.m. the next day.

Outside the courtroom, Prettyman, Grumbach, Howard, and I briefly talked about this turn of events. We agreed that Judge Griesa understood that the plaintiffs were now alleging a completely different agreement than the one originally claimed. Levy's case was collapsing!

"They've changed their case, haven't they?" John asked excitedly as we drove uptown. "Schurtman changed their claim, didn't he?"

"He has," I said. "We've got eight or maybe ten documents where they alleged the same worldwide agreement almost word for word. The judge almost said, 'I don't see how I could find that there was a contract for mail order only,' but he caught himself."

All four of us were elated, smiling. We continued to discuss this new development until we neared our office.

"Would you like to have dinner?" John asked, surprisingly.

"John, we'd love to but we need to put together the copies of the documents containing the original allegations the judge requested," I said. "We also want to review today's transcript carefully when it arrives this evening. Thank you."

"You're welcome," John said. "I understand. We'll see you in the morning."

As we stood on the sidewalk picking up our trial bags, Howard said, "You just turned down a dinner invitation from John Lennon."

"What?" I replied.

"John invited us to have dinner with them and you turned him down," said Howard. I laughed.

"Yeah," I said, "I guess I did." *I really hadn't thought about it like that. We had work to do.*

In the morning John, Yoko, Howard, and I were in a great mood. Judge Griesa interrupted my cross-examination of Levy, who was totally confused, further damaging Levy's claims by his questioning.

Then Prettyman and Grumbach cross-examined him, using the prior complaints and other documents alleging the worldwide agreement that began with his January 9 letter.

Levy's answers about his conversations with Allen Klein were obviously on Judge Griesa's mind. He asked Levy why he'd approved the New York and federal court complaints when they were contrary to what he was saying now.

Schurtman tried to interrupt. The judge shut him down.

"I don't want any comments from you, Mr. Schurtman, at the moment . . . I'm asking the witness," he said.

Levy tried to avoid answering. Prettyman read from his June 1975 deposition in which Levy said he had read the New York complaint, approved its filing, and believed the statements were true. Judge Griesa interrupted yet again:

> THE COURT: Quite frankly, Mr. Levy,
> I am puzzled by the idea of a contract
> that simply dealt with the mail order
> rights and left the retail side of it
> hanging. I just want to tell you that.
> That came as a realization to me last
> night, that that is what we have, and I
> don't quite understand it.

On redirect Schurtman tried to correct Levy's damaging testimony. He began "feeding" answers to Levy with very inaccurate questions about his prior testimony. We objected that Schurtman was improperly "leading" his witness. Judge Griesa agreed.

> THE COURT: I didn't recall [Levy]
> saying that.
> MR. BERGEN: Neither did I, your Honor.
> THE COURT: The record will stand for
> what it stands for. But don't lead him.
> You can't lead him this way.

Schurtman was soon in deeper trouble.

> Q Did Seider ever tell you at one
> point that it would not be necessary to
> go to England [to obtain permission from
> EMI]?
> A Yes. He told me it was not neces-
> sary to go to England.
> THE COURT: I can't permit leading
> [the witness] this way. Again, particu-
> larly, I must tell you, Mr. Schurtman,
> this is so contrary to my memory of the
> record. My memory of the record is I

never understood Mr. Levy to [testify]
that by January 9th or any other date he
thought he had worldwide rights.

No, I don't —

Schurtman interrupted the judge.

MR. SCHURTMAN: He said so in the
letter.

THE COURT: That's the whole point.
Did he write the [January 9] letter
contrary to what he understood and you
can't assume something -- look, please.
The letter is the letter. His testimony
is his testimony.

MR. SCHURTMAN: I'm asking him why he
wrote the letter the way he wrote it.

THE COURT: That's another question.

MR. SCHURTMAN: That was basically my
question.

THE COURT: Why did you write the
[January 9, 1975] letter the way you
wrote it with respect to worldwide
rights?

THE WITNESS: Because I believe the
deal we made I was getting worldwide
rights when it was finally put down in
writing. I would be getting worldwide
rights. The only thing that stopped --

THE COURT: Did you believe that you
had worldwide rights?

THE WITNESS: That I had them already
so I could go and market another country?

THE COURT: Yes, I mean that.

THE WITNESS: No.

```
THE COURT: Okay. Then that's the end
of that.
```

That sounded to me like the end of Morris Levy's bogus case against John Lennon. Court adjourned until the next day when John would be cross-examined.

Chapter 33

Two Virgins Nude Photos—Again?

January 29, 1976
US District Court
New York City

WHEN JOHN AND I PREPARED FOR HIS CROSS-EXAMINATION,
he asked me, "Why didn't Schurtman question me at my deposition?"

"It's a mystery," I replied. "He should have. It borders on
malpractice."

Schurtman made little, if any, headway. He asked John if
he, Seider, or Coury had mentioned that "Mr. Levy claimed
that he had an agreement to make your album" at the January
28 Capitol meeting.

"I don't remember that coming up at all, no," answered
John, adding that he wasn't aware Levy was making such a
claim. (Remember John had not seen Levy's January 9, 1975
letter until I showed it to him on February 3, 1975.) "No, I
don't think anybody was claiming anything then. Mr. Levy
didn't know one way or the other."

John then testified about wanting to sell the album on TV:

> My intentions were tell Capitol and
> EMI that I would like to do that *if it*
> *suited them*. As long as they go out, I
> get paid, anyway. (emphasis added). . .
>
> Well, I mentioned Morris was a front
> runner for TV packaging. I mean, if it

> was going to go on TV, I would have pre-
> ferred Morris to have it.

But Coury made it clear to John that TV marketing of *Rock 'n' Roll* did not suit Capitol or EMI. John testified:

> I don't really remember what was dis-
> cussed about Morris that night because
> my whole thing was about the album and
> the cover and after I had said my bit
> and Al Coury said his bit the night was
> done. We got down to the cover and the
> packaging and billboards and stuff like
> that. I wouldn't, you know, remember it.

John said there were no discussions about the album at Levy's farm.

> Only discussed the music amongst our-
> selves. Three of the musicians had been
> on the original tracks. There was noth-
> ing to discuss [about] the music. It's
> like being in a bath and you don't dis-
> cuss it. You're having a bath.

William Chapman, Schurtman's first witness on January 12, testified John introduced himself at the farm and told him he was making the oldies album for Levy.

I confirmed with John that he had not introduced himself to Chapman or even spoken to him. We knew Schurtman would ask him about it.

Schurtman read that portion of Chapman's testimony and asked John whether he had that conversation with him.

> No, I didn't. I don't introduce my-
> self to people, mainly, because A, they

```
know who I am and B, I'm shy and if
people want to talk to me they come over
and talk.
```

John denied that he and Levy "became personally quite friendly" and that they saw each other "frequently on a social basis [at the Club Cavallero]."

"I was intrigued by him as a character," John testified. "That's one way of putting it . . . Well, to me anything outside of my own house is business. I don't go to dinner with people much for fun." Schurtman tried to get John to admit that he gave Levy a book and autographed it.

"Autographs don't stick in my mind," John replied. "You know I do millions of them . . . I'm not denying I signed the book, but I don't remember it."

We knew John would be questioned about *Roots* and *Two Virgins*.

When we were prepping I told John that Schurtman would ask him about *Two Virgins* in a very negative way.

"He has no idea how you will answer his questions," I said. "Kanzer never asked you about it during your deposition last June."

"He will ask me about it, won't he?" John said. "Well, that's no problem for me to answer and give the reasons why Yoko and I did it. It was called *Unfinished Music No. 1: Two Virgins*. It was part of what turned out to be a trilogy. The second one was *Unfinished Music No. 2: Life with the Lions*. Part of it was recorded in Yoko's room at Queen Charlotte's Hospital in London. She was recovering from a miscarriage. The third part was the *Wedding Album*. It was all very avant-garde stuff. No real music."

We discussed John's concept of *Two Virgins* in detail. By the time we finished, John was ready.

John testified about the "out of focus" photo of him on the *Roots* cover. Schurtman asked him whether he'd ever had any album covers with out of focus photos.

"Offhand, I don't remember. Nothing looked as bad as this," John answered. "I mean I wouldn't use this. It is a lousy picture of me." Schurtman challenged John's statement and John snapped at him.

"It is my opinion and it is my album," he said.

Using the *Roots* cover photo showing John with long hair, Schurtman asked whether the picture showed how he "looked in the winter of 1974 and 1975, before you cut your hair."

"I wish I did," John answered. Schurtman asked when he got his hair cut.

"I tried to do it on New Year's Day," John replied, "but I believe it was the day after."

"Isn't it a fact you cut your hair for purposes of this trial?" Schurtman asked.

"Rubbish," John replied. "I cut it every eighteen months."

Schurtman plunged on, handing John pictures showing how he looked at other times.

"Yes. Different length hair," he answered. "Each picture is a different length."

Judge Griesa lost his patience with Schurtman.

```
    THE COURT: We have business to con-
duct. The main point . . . is that Mr.
Lennon says he did not approve the pre-
sentation of that picture on the Roots
album. Nobody contends that he did.
    Now, that's not even in issue.
```

Schurtman then unwittingly walked into a buzz saw of John's testimony that hurt Levy's case.

```
    Q Now, Mr. Lennon, when you testified
in your direct examination your counsel
put into evidence a photograph of your
other albums, and you testified as to the
pains you personally took in preparing
```

these covers?

A Yes, I believe so.

Q Now, what are your views on the Adam VIII cover?

A I think it is crummy.

Q You think it is in bad taste?

A Yes, I do, very bad taste.

Q Mr. Lennon, we have had here testimony previously about the *Two Virgins* album, which was put out by Tetragramaton [*sic*] because EMI would not handle it?

A Right.

Q At this point I am going to show you that album, Plaintiff's Exhibit 3-A for identification.

I ask you whether you approved that cover?

A Yes, I approved it; I took the photograph myself; I approved every detail of it; I am very proud of it.

Where did you get it? It is very rare.

MR. SCHURTMAN: I offer Plaintiffs' Exhibit 3-A in evidence.

THE WITNESS: This was the one that was being waved around. [John could not resist mentioning Schurtman showing the jury both sides of the cover in the January mistrial.]

THE COURT: Is there any objection?

THE WITNESS: It has the front and back of me and my wife.

MR. BERGEN: No objection, your Honor.

THE COURT: Received.

(Plaintiffs' Exhibit 3-A was received

in evidence.)

Q Were you of the opinion, Mr. Lennon, that this cover enhanced your reputation as an artist?

A Yes, I have no shame about nakedness, and I do not think it is bad taste to be naked, otherwise every artist for the last 2000 years would be on trial for nakedness or having to do with naked bodies. I am a trained art student and nakedness to me is beautiful.

Q Did you run into any problems marketing that album?

A Sir Joseph Lockwood, who was then head of EMI, decided that his company did not want to handle it, only he did not have the guts to tell me to my face, he sent a letter to all his subsidiaries around the world, but he did ask me to autograph the album for him so he could take it home, and it did enhance my reputation, yes.

Q You previously offered to give me an autograph, and with his Honor's permission would you autograph this album for me at the end of the trial?

A It will be a pleasure. It has made me notorious: it is worth a lot of money on the underground.

Q Isn't it a fact that Capitol also refused to handle this album?

A They were instructed by EMI, as far as I remember.

Q Did you, nevertheless, insist that the album be released to the public?

A I could have sent the picture out

without anyone's permission; I did not insist, I said I wanted [it] out, and they did not mind as long as they did not have to handle it.

Q You did arrange for another company, Tetragramaton [*sic*] to put that album out?

A I don't know who came up with Tetragramaton [*sic*]; somebody must have fixed it.

Q But you were interested in getting that album with that cover sold to the public?

A Of course.

Q Do you remember whether there was any adverse publicity when that album got to the music stores?

A There was publicity and we gave an exclusive of the album cover to Rolling Stone, and both Rolling Stone and myself were very happy with the outcome of the publicity.

Q Didn't many music stores refuse to carry this album because they said it was pornographic?

A I don't remember, probably, but they did that with Beatle albums, too.

THE COURT: When did this come out?

THE WITNESS: '68, I think is when it came out. There was a big flurry, and the music in it was avant-garde, they would not have sold it anyway, and it was just screeches and people talking, and it was an event, rather than a musical happening.

• • •

Q There was a big flurry about the
nude album?

A Yes, and I am glad.

Q Why?

A Because it made people think about
their reactions to nudity, including
your own.

Q Not my reactions?

A The whole point of the thing was
to show that a person like me has nothing to hide, and underneath all the fa-
çade and image, I look just like everyone else, and I was well pleased at the
effect of this album on the public . . .
The Americans insisted on putting it in
a brown paper bag; the Europeans were
not so up-tight about it and let it be
released as it stood. So it did go out
somewhere.

Judge Griesa became annoyed at Schurtman's *Two Virgins* questions, explaining the album cover didn't have anything to do with the question of whether Levy and John had entered into a contract. That ended John's testimony after fifty-six pages of cross-examination.

"How do you think it went?" John asked me as we drove uptown.

"You didn't miss a beat," I said. "The time we spent preparing showed up in your answers. I don't think Schurtman scored any points while you scored points for our defense and the counterclaims." I laughed. "When he asked you to autograph *Two Virgins*, he blew up his own 'poor taste' argument!" We all laughed.

"That was quite a mistake, wasn't it?" John asked. "He asked me earlier for an autograph and I told him his daughter already got one. I was surprised then but delighted when he asked me about *Two Virgins*."

John's words, uttered on the stand, reverberated in my mind: *"Where did you get it? It is very rare . . . It will be a pleasure [to autograph* Two Virgins*]. It has made me notorious: it is worth a lot of money on the underground."*

A fitting ending to John's testimony.

Chapter 34

"We [Didn't] Have a Deal"

February 5, 1976
US District Court
New York City

THE TRIAL ON THE BREACH OF CONTRACT CLAIM ended on January 30. Judge Griesa scheduled the final oral argument for 3:00 p.m. February 5.

I advised the judge before we began the oral argument that John and Yoko were unable to be present because they were both ill. They had attended all twelve trial days even though there were only four days when John had to be there because he was testifying. Their interest in the case had to be a very positive sign to Judge Griesa. Morris Levy was not as present as they were.

Since Levy's corporations, Big Seven and Adam VIII, were the plaintiffs, they had the burden of proving Morris Levy and John Lennon had entered into an oral agreement on October 8, 1974. Their federal court complaint alleged that:

"... Lennon would record approximately 15 rock and roll songs, including several songs previously recorded under the production of one Phil Spector, which would be sold as a record and tape under the title '*Roots*' ... by Big Seven or its assignee *on a world wide basis, through mail orders and retail fulfillment centers by means of television merchandising.*" (emphasis added)

In his January 9, 1975 letter to my partner, David Dolgenos, Levy first set forth his worldwide claim. It was repeated seven more times in court documents sworn to or acknowledged by Levy to be true.

Yet now when questioned by Judge Griesa, Levy had sworn that he knew John had not given him the right to sell the album outside the United States or through retail fulfillment centers anywhere. Schurtman conceded this point—again—during the oral argument.

After almost three hours of oral argument, Judge Griesa stated he would issue a written decision soon.

On February 16 I received a gift from John—Bob Gruen's photo of the team, Howard, John, Harold, Yoko, and me having lunch at Sloppy Louie's.

"Thank you for the Sloppy Louie's photo," I told John in a telephone call.

"You're welcome," John said. "I thought you might like to have it as a souvenir for your scrapbook, if you have one."

"I don't keep a scrapbook," I said, "but it's a nice remembrance of our fun lunches at Sloppy Louie's."

"It is, isn't it? When do you think we'll hear from Judge Griesa?"

"It should be very soon. I'll call you when we receive it."

"Thanks," said John. "Until then."

During the case I had reflected on John's deposition testimony about whether Morris was a personal friend. "I wouldn't put it that strongly," John had replied. ". . . I don't have many personal friends. It takes a long time to make a personal friend." I realized that we shared that sentiment, which could explain why we became comfortable with each other.

Late in the afternoon on February 20, Judge Griesa's chambers called. His decision was ready to be picked up. I sent a clerk to the courthouse immediately. Before he returned Grumbach called me. His office was downtown near the courthouse.

"Jay, it's George," he said. "Have a nice weekend, Jay."

"Thanks, George. You, too."

We had won!

By 6:00 p.m. I was holding Judge Griesa's twenty-eight-page opinion in my hand. The victory was total. I was thrilled and excited. So were Howard and Pat. John answered the phone when I called.

"John, I have Judge Griesa's opinion. We won," I said. "Let me read one sentence to you. 'I hold that the plaintiffs have not proved the making of the alleged contract.'"

"We won? We won?" John asked. "That's fabulous. Congratulations, Jay. Thank you for your help."

"Thank you for being so interested in the case and participating in our preparation and attending every day of the trial," I replied. "Your assistance was a big part of the victory." I heard John yell.

"Yoko, Yoko, we won! Jay's on the phone," he said. "The judge said that the plaintiffs hadn't proved that there was a contract."

"Do you want me to tell you some of what the judge said?" I asked.

"Yes, please."

I explained that Judge Griesa spent several pages discussing the "Come Together" settlement, Phil Spector's disappearance with the master tapes, and the exclusive agreements John and The Beatles had with Capitol/EMI. I told him the decision made a number of factual findings that were in our favor.

"He gave little, if any, credence to Levy's claims," I said. "I want to read one of the major findings to you: 'The fact that Levy and the plaintiffs have experienced such difficulty in formulating the terms of the contract for presentation to the court is sufficient in itself to cast doubt on whether there was ever a contract at all.'" I paused to let the words sink in.

"Levy's lies and twists and turns were transparent," I went on. "Since Judge Griesa is the sole finder of fact who observed all the witnesses, that makes an appeal by Morris extremely difficult. This is a big win for you, John. The facts finally caught up with Morris Levy. He has suffered a huge defeat.

"I'll have a copy of the decision delivered to you by messenger. I'm very proud of the job we all did in achieving this victory. Please thank Yoko for her support." (Interestingly, even though Yoko, like John, was present every day of the trial, I could not recall any comment or suggestion she might have made. I believe that she was pleased with the way the trial was proceeding and had no reason to say anything. I'm sure she was supportive with John behind the scenes.)

"Thank you again, Jay," John said.

I was high as a kite. Howard and I called David and Harold Seider about the decision. They, too, were very happy and congratulated us on the win. It was Friday night. Time to go home.

Over the weekend I thought about the trial and the months leading up to January 1976. The whole experience had been exhilarating, stressful, fun, labor intensive and a personal achievement for me. The friendship that John Lennon and I established was important to me. I believe it was important to him also.

John was happy, relaxed, and "chilled out." He and Yoko had reunited when John and I met. She became pregnant and John withdrew from the world in almost every sense. Music was put on a shelf for the first time in decades. He didn't even know who Freddie Mercury was! John just wanted to be a father to Sean, his new son.

But he was "into" *Big Seven and Adam VIII v. John Lennon*. John was available and 100 percent present when I needed him. We had worked together closely to map out his testimony. We had educated Judge Griesa, the musician, about John Lennon, the artist; The Beatles; John's recording studio expertise; the finalization of the *Rock 'n' Roll* album; and the damage John suffered as a result of the bootleg *Roots* album. It was a very personal victory for him.

Chapter 35

One Down, Two to Go

February 27, 1976
New York City

THE MONDAY AFTER JUDGE GRIESA DISMISSED the plaintiffs' claims, he scheduled a hearing for 1:30 p.m. February 27. I called John to let him know.

"Congratulations and thank you again, Jay," John said. "Yoko and I read the decision a couple of times. The judge wrote a very good decision for us. He didn't buy any of Morris's story."

"No, he didn't," I replied. "He'll appeal but it'll be difficult to overturn. The appellate court would have to find that the decision was 'clearly erroneous,' given the evidence. I don't believe that can happen.

"The judge has scheduled a hearing this Friday afternoon. He wants to set a trial date on the counterclaims asserted by you and Capitol. You don't need to attend the hearing. You'll be our witness on the counterclaims."

"When do you think the trial will begin?" John asked.

"It'll depend on Judge Griesa's calendar. I'll call you after the hearing. How's Sean? Getting bigger, I'll bet?"

"He's wonderful," John answered. "He's growing. We have a lot of fun with him. I've been taking him to the park so we can get some fresh air."

"Great," I said. "Give my best to Yoko."

Friday's hearing evolved into a long discussion about the evidence John Lennon and Capitol/EMI would introduce.

Capitol/EMI would prove the release of *Roots* had caused *Rock 'n' Roll* to lose sales. John's reduced royalties would be calculated using Capitol's album sales.

As for the damage to John's reputation and career, Judge Griesa stated he'd need evidence of such damage.

> THE COURT: . . . I am just saying if you want to get damages on the basis that there was some impairment inflicted upon Mr. Lennon in some way because of the release of this album that was not finally edited, you leave it the way you think it ought to be left, but if for any reason you want to prove that there is a difference in the quality of the music, no matter how subtle, no matter how obvious or whatever, I am just suggesting I am not in a position to make much of a finding because I heard this quickly with an ear that probably is not as trained as it should be, and that is all there is to it. That is all I am saying to you. You decide what you want to do.
>
> MR. BERGEN: That is basically the testimony that I was talking about that we would want to put on.
>
> THE COURT: Okay. I will just expound -- I don't go into this form of music, but I do a lot of listening, I am very interested in music, and my feeling is I have had some occasion to go into this subtle difference, freezing, touch, et cetera, but they are not going to be recognized by the listener in those terms; the listener is not going to sit there and say, unless he is an expert,

'Well, this phrase should have consisted
of three notes, instead of four notes.'
   But all of those differences make up
to an impact on a listener. It is the
difference between a lively performance
and a dull performance, that kind of
thing. So I am prepared to realize the
importance of the most small differences,
but I just have to have it made plain.

Schurtman wasn't present for this important hearing. Kanzer asked Judge Griesa for permission to amend Big Seven's claim against John to assert that he'd breached the "Come Together" settlement by failing to record "Angel Baby" on *John Lennon Rock 'n' Roll*. Big Seven wanted the opportunity to prove damages in the form of lost publishing royalties.

We agreed to the amendment so we could dispose of the claim. After the trial on Capitol/EMI's and John's counterclaims, evidence would be introduced on Big Seven's claim.

"I have the transcript of the hearing," I told John when I called him. "We'll start March 17. The judge commented about the evidence he expects to hear to prove damages.

"He is going to award damages to Capitol/EMI and you. He ruled that Levy had no right to release *Roots* and he'll award damages as a result of that. That's no longer in doubt. Capitol's evidence will be the key to the damages he awards for lost sales of *Rock 'n' Roll*. The damages awarded to you will flow from that amount and based on the illegal use of your name and likeness under New York law.

"Can I read you a couple of paragraphs from the transcript?" I asked.

"Sure," John replied. I read some of the judge's musings about what evidence he would need to calculate a dollar figure for damages.

"That's interesting," John replied. "He said he was very interested in music and that he listens to music a lot. That'll be helpful in planning what we'll introduce, won't it?"

"It will," I replied. "You'll testify, but we'll need someone else to testify about the differences between *Roots* and *Rock 'n' Roll.* Do you agree?"

"Yes," John said.

"I'm going to call Chet Flippo at *Rolling Stone*," I said. "He can recommend one of their rock music critics to speak to me. I'll let you know what I find out."

Chet transferred me to Dave Marsh. When I explained I was representing John Lennon in the Morris Levy case, he agreed to meet me that afternoon in his office. I brought the *Roots* and *Rock 'n' Roll* albums with me.

"Would you be willing to listen to these two albums?" I asked Dave. "*Roots* is the one Morris Levy illegally released. The court ruled last week that Levy and his companies didn't have an agreement with John permitting them to release *Roots*. Now John and Capitol have the opportunity to present evidence on their counterclaims against Levy, starting March 17."

I explained he would testify about the differences between the two albums.

"John's basic claim is that *Roots* damaged his reputation," I said. "Morris Levy produced it from a 7-1/2 ips reel-to-reel tape of the unfinished album John gave him.

"Our position is that the *Roots* tracks weren't the finished album. Record albums by a major artist like John are made from 15 ips master tapes, not 7-1/2 ips tapes. *Roots* has two tracks that John eliminated from *Rock 'n' Roll* because of their poor quality. And, finally, the *Roots* cover is cheesy and nowhere near John's or The Beatles' high standards."

I told Dave that Judge Griesa was an accomplished classical harpsichordist who listens to a lot of music, but not rock and roll.

"That's why we need you to help us explain the poor quality of *Roots*."

"I'd be glad to listen to the albums and testify," Dave replied. "Sounds interesting."

I thanked him and handed him the two albums. We agreed to talk in a few days. I called John and told him about the meeting.

The next afternoon a messenger delivered a two-page, single-spaced letter to me from Dave, which stated he compared *Roots* and *Rock 'n' Roll*, track for track. The letter sharply criticized *Roots*, including its "package." I hadn't asked Dave to critique *Roots*, but I was happy to receive such a detailed letter. Clearly, he'd given *Roots* a lot of thought. I called John.

"I just received a two-page letter from Dave Marsh that rips *Roots* to shreds," I told him. "It's an excellent letter for us. I'll send a copy by messenger."

"What does it say?" John asked.

"I'll read the first sentence. It reads like your testimony in January. 'The quality of the sound is simply shoddy.' It's all downhill from there.

"I'll meet with Dave to discuss his testimony. Capitol will spend several days presenting evidence. Your testimony and Dave's will follow. We'll meet before you testify. You and Yoko are going to come on March 17, aren't you?"

"Yes, we want to be there."

Chapter 36

Levy Disappears

March 17, 18, 30, 1976
US District Court
New York City

JOHN AND YOKO ARRIVED IN MY OFFICE at 10:30 a.m. on March 17. We wished each other a happy Saint Patrick's Day and talked briefly about the day ahead and how Sean was.

"What's in the jar?" I asked John, who was holding a quart jar.

"Garlic juice," he replied. "We've started drinking it. It has lots of vitamins, aids your immune system, and has many other benefits. Yoko discovered how healthy it is."

"May I smell it?"

"Sure," he replied, handing me the jar. I opened it and took a whiff. "That'll clean out your sinuses, but I'm not sure I'd want to drink it." I handed it back. Fortunately, he didn't ask me to taste it.

At the courthouse we entered Room 506, our home for a couple of days. Prettyman called Bhaskar Menon, president of Capitol Records Inc., as his first witness. Menon testified all day and part of the next morning.

He was followed by Don Zimmerman, Capitol's executive vice president and chief operating officer. Zimmerman, who'd been senior vice president of marketing in February 1975, testified for the remainder of March 18 and part of March 30. Harold Posner, Capitol's director of financial planning and analysis, testified for the remainder of March 30 and the next morning.

All three supported Capitol's claim that *Roots* reduced *Rock 'n' Roll* sales, damaging Capitol's bottom line. They proved that TV advertising and mail-order sales of *Roots*, begun on February 7, forced Capitol to move up *Rock 'n' Roll's* release date to February 13.

The rushed *Rock 'n' Roll* release meant Capitol's advertising and marketing program markedly truncated its efforts supporting the album, reducing sales. Since *Walls and Bridges* had been released in mid-September 1974, only five months earlier, the forced early release of *Rock 'n' Roll* also created a bottleneck: too much John Lennon product in the market. A third factor causing lost sales was confusion in the minds of John's fans and the public as to which album was the official one.

On March 30, Schurtman stated he had no further questions for Zimmerman. The judge permitted me to have Zimmerman identify a cassette containing TV commercials for four of John's albums—*Mind Games*, *Walls and Bridges*, *Rock 'n' Roll*, and *Shaved Fish*.

    MR. BERGEN: Your Honor, if I might
just play the commercials. Because they
are going to come through the machine
later on.
    MR. SCHURTMAN: I don't know what is
the relevance of these commercials.
    THE COURT: You mean for all these al-
bums?
    MR. BERGEN: Your Honor, the relevance
is that Mr. Lennon's counterclaims one
of the things he has complained about is
that the *Roots* commercial was not up to
his standards and I would like to show
the Court four commercials for Mr. Lennon's albums and Mr. Lennon tomorrow
will testify as to what role he played
in those commercials. They are very

brief, they are 30 seconds each.

MR. SCHURTMAN: Is that supposed to establish a basis for damages? And if so, how?

MR. PRETTYMAN: Can we argue that later?

MR. SCHURTMAN: I would like to know what the relevancy of the offer is.

THE COURT: We have gotten this thing of comparing the *Roots* album with his albums and I would think by the same token, we can compare the commercial with his own commercials. Isn't that the issue in the case?

MR. SCHURTMAN: I don't think it is, but if you want to accept it, I will object to it for the record.

MR. BERGEN: The other point is that --

THE COURT: I will approve it. Television set playing.

We played the four commercials.

THE COURT: I don't have any particular memory of the Rock and Roll, of the *Roots* commercial. Have you got that around?

MR. BERGEN: We have it right here.

(Commercial played on the television.)

John's commercials were admitted into evidence. I had a surprise for Schurtman.

I reminded Zimmerman that he earlier testified, when asked by Schurtman, that reviews of *Rock 'n' Roll* were "not

good." Responding to a question from me Zimmerman testified that Grand Funk Railroad was a band that received "uni-
versally bad reviews" their first three years on Capitol. Zimmerman said their reviews "were negative and in the strongest
sense of the word," adding that he didn't "recall seeing one
favorable review in the first three years."

Despite the fact that the band's records generated "very
little interest, particularly from the top 40 radio stations" and
that they never had a hit single, Zimmerman said that Grand
Funk's first album sold 700,000–800,000 copies and their next
seven albums sold more than 1 million copies each.

After Schurtman's brief cross, Zimmerman was excused
and Posner testified until court adjourned.

"'They were negative and in the strongest sense of the
word,'" said Howard, loudly laughing as he quoted Zimmerman. I laughed, too, as the limo pulled away from the courthouse.

"What was all that about Grand Funk Railroad?" John
asked. "How did you come up with that band?"

"Don't you remember?" I replied. "I told you that I had
represented Terry Knight, Grand Funk's former manager. The
band split from Terry or vice versa. There was litigation."

"Yes, I remember now," John said.

"When Schurtman was making a big deal about the negative reviews, I started thinking about Grand Funk's early history," I said. "Their music was barely listenable. Reviews were
terrible. They couldn't get radio play. Terry recognized that and,
with Capitol's help, played it up. Through touring and other
tactics, the band developed a cult following, especially in the
deep South.

"Terry promoted one of their albums on a Times Square
billboard," I continued. "The billboard sign installers went on
strike. Grand Funk's ad was up there for months. They filled
arenas. I got involved in December 1972. They sold out Madison Square Garden. Their albums consistently went platinum.
Their fans thought it was a badge of honor to support them

because of the bad reviews and no airplay.

"I thought we could pull a fast one on Schurtman because he wouldn't be able to figure out how we picked Grand Funk. It worked."

"It did," said John, laughing.

I met with John and Dave Marsh between March 18 and March 30. I also arranged for a Record Plant engineer to install a turntable and sound system with speakers in Judge Griesa's courtroom for use on March 31.

We would have to play *Roots* and *Rock 'n' Roll* when Dave testified.

We played records sooner than I thought. On March 31, John and Judge Griesa ad-libbed a surprise.

Chapter 37

The Pop and Avant-Garde Artist

March 31, 1976
US District Court
New York City

SCHURTMAN CROSS-EXAMINED POSNER about John Lennon albums that were "truly representative Lennon albums" and how many copies each had sold. Judge Griesa interrupted.

> THE COURT: Would it be possible to --
> I don't have any particular feel of the
> character of the music -- is there any
> way that we can give -- play something
> to illustrate the character of these dif-
> ferent albums?

Rock wasn't Judge Griesa's kind of music, but he was obviously itching to hear John's solo albums to expand his musical experience and knowledge. John and I had hoped for just this situation in January. We hadn't anticipated, however, that the judge would want to delve into John's solo career in depth.

After more questions, the judge interrupted again.

> THE COURT: Do you regard *Some Time in
> New York City* as not a typical [Lennon]
> album?
> THE WITNESS: Yes, your Honor.
> THE COURT: I mean, what is it that

makes something typical or untypical?

    THE WITNESS: I think the best, if
I might say, sir, would be to kind of
listen to it yourself. I didn't mean it
quite that way.

    THE COURT: That's why I thought it
would be a good idea. In other words, it
depends on the music or the lyrics or
something in the content, right?

    THE WITNESS: Yes, sir.

Posner's answers were perfect. He understood that Judge Griesa was very curious about the solo albums. Their colloquy led to a three-way discussion among the judge, me, and Schurtman about three of the albums issued before *Some Time In New York City*, specifically *Unfinished Music No. 2: Life with the Lions*, *The Wedding Album*, and *Live Peace in Toronto*. Judge Griesa made a request of Schurtman who'd brought the albums to court.

    THE COURT: Play them all in order [in
sequence of release].

· · ·

    THE COURT: I am not going to hear the
whole thing but somebody ought to have
an idea of what is representative here.

Schurtman played side one of *Unfinished Music No. 2: Life with the Lions*, featuring John Lennon and Yoko Ono.

    MR. BERGEN: There aren't any tracks
on this side. It just says one, Cam-
bridge 1969.

    THE COURT: All right.

```
        (Music played)
        MR. BERGEN: There are no other --
there is just - there aren't tracks on
this, there aren't different songs.
        THE COURT: Just don't get worried,
Mr. Bergen. It doesn't hurt to play a
little music.
```

I wasn't. It was great he wanted to hear John's music.

After playing some music on the reverse side of *Unfinished Music No. 2,* the *Wedding Album* was next. We only had a cassette tape in court, though, not a record, so we couldn't play it. Schurtman moved to *Live Peace in Toronto.*

```
        THE COURT: Is this Rock or what is
it?
        MR. SCHURTMAN: That is what I wanted
to ask.
        MR. LENNON: It is all rock.
```

John called out his answer from the spectator section. Startled, I turned to look at him. *Too much. Our main witness is testifying from his courtroom seat. He's not on the witness stand.*

```
        THE COURT: This is not rock and roll?
        MR. BERGEN: That is an old rock and
roll song from the 1950s that was made
famous by a singer named Carl Perkins.
        THE COURT: What is the name of the
song?
        MR. BERGEN: "Blue Suede Shoes."
        MR. LENNON: And Elvis Presley. [John
had to make sure Elvis got his due.]
```

•   •   •

```
     THE COURT: In other words, there's
one rock and roll song on there?
     MR. BERGEN: There are several.
     The other distinguishing factor,
aside from what you are about to hear,
which makes this album a lot like --
     THE COURT: It is very important to me
to understand what the songs are.
     (Music playing)
     MR. BERGEN: Can we put Mr. Lennon on
the witness stand?
     THE COURT: Could you come up?
     MR. LENNON: Yes, sure.
     Am I still sworn?
```

Very cool, John, I thought.

```
     THE COURT: You are still sworn.
     (Mr. Posner temporarily excused)
```

Given Judge Griesa's interest, suggesting that John take the stand seemed the thing to do. I hadn't expected it but I wasn't concerned because I knew he could handle whatever happened next.

```
     JOHN LENNON, resumed:
     THE COURT: The first piece we played,
Live Peace in Toronto, what is the name
of that?
     THE WITNESS: "Blue Suede Shoes," and
it is a '50's rock and roll song similar
to the Rock and Roll album and Roots,
similar kind of material, the only dif-
ference being that this was a live con-
cert.
     THE COURT: I see.
```

Now are there other rock and roll
songs on that album?

THE WITNESS: There are two others,
sort of standard rock and roll songs
from the '50's.

MR. SCHURTMAN: Do you want to hear
them?

THE WITNESS: Shall I just --

THE COURT: Just a second. [To Schurtman, stopping him from breaking in.]

THE WITNESS: Finish these questions?

The other songs on the record are either written by myself or Yoko. Side Two
is in fact Yoko singing. I wouldn't term
it rock and roll, sort of avant-garde
mixed with rock and roll.

MR. BERGEN: Can we just get on the
record, what the other two rock and roll
songs are?

THE WITNESS: There is one called
"Money." And there is one called "Dizzy Miss Lizzy," which I had previously
recorded with The Beatles. But I re-
recorded it at this live concert just
because I knew the song.

THE COURT: OK.

Can you just explain to me what the
difference between rock and roll and rock
is?

THE WITNESS: It is the same.

THE COURT: It is the same?

THE WITNESS: You see, when people say
rock and roll, they tend to be thinking about the '50's, but practically any
record that is on the radio, it could be
called rock and roll.

The term has broadened over the
years. Actually it is a specific type of
music, but you call anything with a beat
rock and roll music. They just call it
rock for convenience rather than rock
and roll.

THE COURT: Could you start the album
over and play a little bit of the three
rock and roll songs?

After the judge listened to "Blue Suede Shoes," "Money,"
and "Dizzy Miss Lizzy," John explained that "[t]he first side
is all straight songs, the second side gets a bit wild." After the
record ended Judge Griesa resumed his questions.

THE COURT: Just for curiosity, when
you produce a record of a concert, do
you edit it and go through the same
things that you told me about [in the
January trial]?

THE WITNESS: Yes, you have less scope
because a lot of it leaks on. You can't
separate the tracks and beneath so you
have a harder time with it. If there is
nothing there to work with — but you can
do quite a lot of work in the studio.

Judge Griesa was getting an education from John not only
about studio recording but repairing a live concert recording in
the studio.

Schurtman had a question.

"Your Honor, could we ask Mr. Lennon what the Plastic
Ono Band is?"

THE WITNESS: Be happy to explain.
Plastic Ono Band is a conceptual group,

it doesn't exist, meaning that whoever plays with either myself or myself and my wife or Yoko separately is called the Plastic Ono Band, meaning if we make a record now in the courtroom, and we just sang together, I would call that Plastic Ono Band. So anybody is the Plastic Ono Band, even the audience. That's why Capitol can't sign them up.

Judge Griesa next wanted to hear the album, *Plastic Ono Band*.

THE WITNESS: That's the *Mother* album, it's got a tree on the front, and me sitting under the tree.

If it helps, I refer to that album as Mother because it's got a song on it called "Mother" and everybody got confused because I never gave it a title, so we called it Mother for short.

This album was the first solo album I made after leaving The Beatles that wasn't either with my wife or avant-garde. This is the first straight album.

MR. GRUMBACH [Apple's lawyer]: The first track is "Mother."

(Music played)

MR. SCHURTMAN: Do you want me to move it on?

THE COURT: OK.

THE WITNESS: That's just a straight album.

MR. SCHURTMAN: Your Honor, could we ask Mr. Lennon whether he wrote this song?

THE WITNESS: Yes.

MR. SCHURTMAN: That is something you wrote?

THE WITNESS: Yes, unless it is stipulated, most of it will be written by me, yes. It is all written by me. I think maybe Yoko helped me on one song or something. I would have to look at the credits. In general, I guess I wrote them all.

THE COURT: Now when you say you wrote it, you wrote the lyrics?

THE WITNESS: And the music, yes. I always do both, yes.

• • •

(Music played)

THE COURT [after the record is flipped to side two]: Why don't you play the last one on this side?

(Music played)

THE COURT: The very last one.

(Music played)

MR. BERGEN: Can we just have on the record that that song ["My Mummy's Dead"] is 48 seconds long?

THE COURT: All right.

THE COURT: Now the next one is --

MR. SCHURTMAN: The next one is "Imagine," the big one.

MR. BERGEN: One side [of the album's paper sleeve] has the lyrics, the other side has who appeared on the album.

(Music played)

In explaining the span of his music, John likened *Imagine*, released in 1971, to a "full-length feature film." Next came his double album, *Some Time in New York City*, issued in June 1972: one record featured an avant-garde performance with Frank Zappa "that goes into madness," John said, while the other was political.

"I look at the political rock side as a documentary," John testified.

Next came *Mind Games* in 1973. According to John, it was a transition album in which he resumed writing so-called normal rock songs, just like an artist might switch from one style to another.

"At the time," he told Judge Griesa, "just like a painter, you would see him coming out of his blue phase into his pink phase, and it was neither blue nor pink, it was sort of blink."

The court recessed until 2:15 p.m.

I noticed Dave Marsh in the courtroom and introduced him to John, Yoko, and Howard.

"Would you like to join us for lunch?" John asked Dave.

"I would," he replied.

"Great," John said. "There's a wonderful seafood restaurant we like nearby."

"That was quite a surprise," I said as we drove to Sloppy Louie's. "Do you know what was great about your testimony today, John, aside from the fact that you weren't supposed to testify?"

"No, what?" he asked.

"I almost laughed out loud when you chimed in from the audience, 'It is all rock,'" I said. "When I realized how hot the judge was to understand your songs, I decided, shoot, let's get him on the stand."

"That was pretty good, wasn't it?" John asked. "I knew I could connect again with the judge the way we did in January. There weren't any questions he or Schurtman would ask me that I wouldn't be able to answer. We were talking about albums Yoko and I made and albums I made."

"You explained everything very clearly," I said. "Good job."

When we arrived at Sloppy Louie's, we sat at our usual corner table.

"How long have you been at *Rolling Stone*?" John asked Dave.

"Since last June. I'd previously written for *Creem* and *Newsday*, the Long Island paper."

"You didn't know the judge was going to ask about John's music, did you?" Dave asked me.

"No, we didn't," I replied, "but we know he's really interested in learning about John's music from the January trial. Right, John?"

"He is," John said. "He really likes it when he and I get into a conversation about the music. He doesn't know anything about rock and roll, but Jay said that he mentioned at a hearing last month that he listens to a lot of music. So we knew he would probably ask lots of questions."

"He'll do the same with you, Dave," I said. "He'll ask questions and all you have to do is give straightforward answers, as if you were being interviewed. The judge is really into the music, John's music, so just follow him wherever he wants to go."

"You really don't know what he's going to ask me?" Dave said.

"No," I replied, "but that's okay because you can educate him about rock and roll. This is your area of expertise, right?"

"It is," Dave said.

"Then you'll have as much fun as John is having when you testify."

As usual, no one bothered John or Yoko while we ate.

During the recess Granett, Capitol's lawyer, had acquired a disc copy of the *Wedding Album*. It was marked as Defendant's Exhibit CB-6 and admitted into evidence.

The avant-garde *Wedding Album*, an elaborate collector's item, comes in a 12" x 12" x 1/2" white box. The top features a photo of John and Yoko on March 20, 1969, as they leave a white government building in the City and Garrison of Gibraltar after their marriage. Dressed in white, they're standing on the top step of a staircase under an arch. A certified copy of their marriage certificate is pasted on the inside of the box's top.

Inside the box is a foldout record jacket featuring a large photo of John and Yoko and the album, which consists mostly of people talking—snippets of interviews with reporters, for instance, and a John and Yoko call-and-response duet over the sound of their own heartbeats. Another foldout displays their wedding pictures, press clippings, and photos of John and Yoko's widely publicized weeklong Bed-In for Peace at the Amsterdam Hilton.

We played both sides to show Judge Griesa that the *Wedding Album* contained no "regular songs," as he called them.

In a discussion with Schurtman, Judge Griesa made the point that John's albums and songs didn't fit a rigid pattern. They were different because John tries different ways of expressing himself as an artist and in making music. The judge also indicated that, as far as he was concerned, this variety was a plus.

Judge Griesa then asked John to describe *Shaved Fish* "[a]ny way you want to."

John called the compilation album "a repackage," meaning the album comprised songs that had been released as singles in the previous five or six years. Some had appeared on albums while others, such as "Happy Christmas (War is Over)" and "Instant Karma," hadn't.

When Judge Griesa asked him to characterize the singles, John said that most were "normal" rock but that two, including a shortened "Woman Is the Nigger of the World," were political. He hadn't been entirely satisfied with his lyrics on "Woman" the first time it aired.

```
     THE COURT: What is the total number of
songs?
     THE WITNESS: 11 and the Reprise. There
```

is "Give Peace a Chance" twice. That is one.

MR. SCHURTMAN: Between 11 and 12.

BY MR. SCHURTMAN

Q "Give Peace a Chance" you would say is sort of political?

A Yes, because it is in a different frame of mind to "Power of [*sic*] the People."

Q What kind of song is "Cold Turkey"?

A It is just a song.

Q Rock and roll?

A Well, they are all rock and rolls; some are political rock and roll. Everything I do is rock and roll.

Q You count "Mind Games" and "Imagine" in there?

A "Imagine" is a slow rock number.

Q Do you distinguish between country style rock and hard rock?

A There are so many degrees. We can go on forever. But in general I call it rock.

Q Let's go back to Shaved Fish. What style is "Instant Karmar [*sic*]"?

A You know what karmar [*sic*] is. [John looks at the judge.]

THE COURT: No.

THE WITNESS: It is an eastern thing, karmar [*sic*]. We are all here because of Makar [*sic*]. It is just a song.

Q What is "Power to the People"?

A That is a definite political one.

Q And "Mother"?

A I would call that autobiographical.

Q "Woman is the Nigger of the World"?

230

A That would be political.

Q "Imagine" is what you call slow rock?

A Yes, with a little politics, but not with sugar in it. It is hard to describe.

Q And "Whatever Gets You Through The Night"?

A That is easy come, easy go.

Q *"Mind Games"*?

A That is just rock and roll.

Q "No. 9 Dream"?

A Rock and roll.

Q "Happy Christmas War is Over"?

A That is a little touch of each, perhaps, although it is namely a Christmas song, it does have a little catch line about the war is over. You could see [*sic*] it is a peace song.

Q How about the little legend on the cover, 'A conspiracy of silence speaks louder than words'? Is that a political slogan?

A No, that is philosophy, and you will find a statement on each record I make either by me or a friend of mine.

MR. SCHURTMAN: Do you want to hear any other records at this point?

THE COURT: No. You can step down. Finish with Mr. Posner.

(Witness excused.)

Schurtman continued to cross-examine Posner until court adjourned.

"I wonder whether the judge is getting annoyed with Schurtman interrupting your chats with him," I said to John in the limo. "The judge loves to ask you questions about this music that is a mystery to him. He's hooked on it, isn't he?"

"He really does like talking about it and trying to understand what I've done," John replied. "I enjoy the back-and-forth, too. Schurtman doesn't understand that breaking in doesn't stop the judge from questioning me."

"It went very well today," I said. "Schurtman's just wasting time at this point."

I told John Capitol's case would end with Posner's testimony. Then he and Dave would testify.

"I don't think your testimony is going to take that long," I said. "You testified in January about the crummy *Roots* album and how you were damaged by it. You won't have any trouble with Schurtman on cross-examination, right?"

"No," John replied. "We've been over this a lot."

"Schurtman's angry and it's showing," I said. "He took a beating from Judge MacMahon. He thought he'd stopped the trial in January by waving around the *Two Virgins* cover, but we got a new judge in a few hours and then he got tricked into waiving a jury. Then he didn't like you and Judge Griesa becoming musical buddies in January, and he lost Levy's bogus breach of contract claim. So use your witty sarcasm on him during cross-examination."

"I'll have some fun with him," John said. "I don't think he realizes how angry I am about Morris getting us involved in this mess. Yoko and I have been here every day because we want the judge to know that winning this case is very important to us."

"Good. Continue to answer questions the way you think they should be answered," I urged John. "The judge wants to hear your testimony, your version of events, your explanations. Schurtman will continue to jump up and down, objecting, but the judge is going to ignore him. You just keep doing what you've been doing. It's great!"

John and Yoko dropped Howard and me at our office. That's how we ended March 31.

Chapter 38

The Crummy *Roots* Album

April 1, 1976
US District Court
New York City

WHEN JOHN TESTIFIED IN THE MORNING, he explained that the rush to release *Rock 'n' Roll* prevented him from working with Chuck Braverman on a live commercial. John said he'd used Braverman, an award-winning filmmaker, to make other album commercials. As he described his idea for *Rock 'n' Roll*, Judge Griesa had questions.

THE WITNESS: My idea of the commercial for the Rock and Roll was a parody of the Chubby Checker TV commercial, he being a rock and roll singer in the early '60s, and it was on so many times over the last five years, it became a joke. Everybody knows the commercial. There was one other commercial that was famous, the 7-Up [*sic*] commercial in that period where the guy with greased hair and a leather jacket says, "Do you remember when?"

And then they go back to the '50s, where there is no 7-Up [*sic*] and only Coca-Cola.

So I had this idea of combining both

of these commercials somehow. The Chubby Checker one had people dancing in '50s clothes; the 7-Up [sic] had a guy with greased hair and a leather jacket, and he turns around very corny and says, "Hi, remember me," he says.

THE COURT: That was the 7-Up [sic] commercial?

THE WITNESS: Yes, it was a sort of classic commercial, and I was going to do, "Hi, remember me," as if I was already dead and gone. Then I told Braverman about it, either I or through Tony King, and Braverman got excited and sent back a whole pile of images that he had about a juke box and how you had this '50 car, a Cadillac, and he was going to make the whole set, and I was to go to the West Coast to play the lead in the commercial, and Ringo and two friends, Ringo Starr and a few other friends from the business were going to all gather in the background and be the dancers, without being announced they were famous people, just in the back of the commercial, these people would be dancing and there would be Harry Nilsson and Ringo Starr and a few friends from the business, but that never happened. So I had to tell Chuck that I can't come down to do it and he is going to have to use his rather inventive head again and make something, a still picture of that.

In response to a Schurtman lack of relevance objection, Judge Griesa commented: "There is no problem, and as far as the relevance, he is describing what he had planned to do on his commercial. I don't know how anything could be more relevant to what his claim is."

I resumed my questioning.

Q What was the reason that you couldn't do this commercial the way you had planned?

A Because Morris came out with his album and Capitol said, 'Let's go ahead.' There was no time. They certainly wanted to put the album out, and so they put it out and there was no time to make a decent commercial or a better one.

• • •

Q In other words, the Rock and Roll commercial, instead of being live, was animation.

A He had to use stills again, like a still picture of the album cover, and I recall there his cartoon figure in it, and for the short space of time you had to make it, it was a attractive commercial, but it could have been much more interesting.

• • •

Q Have you ever listened to the *Roots* album?

A No.

Q Do you have to listen to it to know what is wrong with it?

A No.

                    •   •   •

THE COURT: Everybody has been reluctant
to have me hear music.

MR. BERGEN: Mr. Marsh from Rolling
Stone magazine will go through the albums.

John then explained how *Roots* had damaged his reputation.

A Firstly, because it came out in
such a hurry that there was no preparation for the marketing of the commercial.

THE COURT: He is asking you about the
Roots album.

THE WITNESS: That damaged me by making my own album have to come out too
quickly. It came out on the tail of
Walls and Bridges, which had only been
out four or five months, and generally I
leave a nine- or twelve-month period between albums, and albums do go on selling for longer than four or five months.
It just made me look bad.

The commercial Levy put on TV was
atrocious and ugly and cheap. It made me
look cheap. The album itself they put
out made me look cheap by its content,
by putting out stuff that I would never
put out, two tracks especially.

Q You are referring to "Angel Baby"
and "Be My Baby"?

A Yes. It confused the public's

mind, was the main thing.

MR. SCHURTMAN: I object. This witness is not qualified to tell us how the public was confused.

THE WITNESS: I am. I met the public, who talked to me about my product. I met a taxi driver who said, "Sorry, I already bought the wrong one." That is the public. They talk to me on the street. I know what they are thinking. I don't live in some ivory tower. I walk the streets. I get in taxicabs and I know what they think.

THE COURT: I won't accept any more evidence on this point.

Let us go back. What did you experience or hear?

THE WITNESS: Well, people were confused as to (a) What I was doing on a TV commercial and (b) When the Capitol album came out they didn't know which was which and it just was confusing to have two products out. It is like having two shows opening at the same time, somebody is opening up with the rough print of the movie in the Village, and the main movie is trying to be shown uptown, they are advertising both movies, and people don't know which movie to go to; they don't know they are getting a lousy print. They think because it has my name on it I endorsed it.

I don't know how else to say it. They were confused by it, and the industry was confused. I think I looked like a fool in the industry, still do. I am

still being hailed [*sic*] into court, I
am still being here; people say, "Are
you still messing around with Morris
Levy?" It is humiliation from the word
"go" and it is not good for my career,
especially since I am re-negotiating
contracts.

• • •

Q Did you have any specific conversations with any member of the public
about this confusion?

A I honestly remember one taxi driver talking to me after I had been on a
radio program. Some members of the public rang up the radio station and they
were confused on it, WNEW, when I was
promoting the Rock and Roll album on
WNEW. I did not have time to do my usual
promotion on the Rock and Roll album. I
usually go to the West Coast and Capitol arranges for me to do certain interviews, either by telephone or in person
with key members of the press, and where
you do a promotion on an album you talk
about the album to people and on radio,
and there was no time for all that.

• • •

Q Mr. Lennon, do you place great
importance on the use of your name and
picture and likeness?

A Inasmuch as that is what I earn my
money with.

```
Q  Have you ever endorsed any product
other than your own products or records
of The Beatles?
A  As far as I remember, The Beatles
and myself only promoted our own stuff.
```

The judge ended John's direct testimony.

```
THE COURT: All right, cross-examine.
```

Mr. Schurtman's brief cross-examination before the lunch recess focused on Capitol's decision to rush the *Rock 'n' Roll* release.

At Sloppy Louie's we discussed the *Roots* TV commercial. John described in detail why it was cheesy. "I know how to answer any questions about the commercial," John said. "I saw it twice. It was awful."

John testified he'd seen the commercial "a couple of times" and objected to the "dreadful cover . . . the other pictures they selected . . . were [not] favorable to me . . . Morris Levy didn't have much time to make that either . . . it has nothing different about it from any other tinpot selling oldies but goldies, on TV . . . [i]t had no inventiveness . . . I try to make my commercials stand out a little . . . if I have pictures going out, I would like to have nice pictures. It is part of the music business. It is called your image."

Schurtman spent a lot of time questioning John about a photo he had used for the cover of *Unfinished Music No. 2: Life with the Lions.* It depicted John and Yoko walking out of court. They had been arrested in London in 1968 for possession of hash. Schurtman was trying to show that John's reputation could not be damaged by *Roots* because John chose that photo for an album cover.

After Schurtman showed John a photo somewhat similar to the album cover photo John testified, "That is not the picture I chose [for my cover]. That is a different picture, see?

. . .That's the difference between Mona Lisa smiling and Mona Lisa not smiling."

Schurtman then tried to show that John's fans wouldn't know whether one of his albums contained some avant-garde music, only avant-garde music, or no real music at all. John explained that *Unfinished Music No. 2: Life with the Lions*, "was a follow-up to Two Virgins, which is Unfinished Music No. 1, and it went on a Zapa [*sic*] label [which] always put out avant-garde music by a guy called John Tavener and Zapa [*sic*] was avant-garde." John continued stating that if fans saw a Lennon record in a store they "would be entitled to assume that it is a Lennon record. My fans know me well. They know they are liable to get anything from bag-pipes to rock and roll."

In response to a question by the judge about *Two Virgins*, John stated: "We are not singing; it is completely avant-garde. There is a live performance of Yoko, and it is just me on the guitar playing."

When Schurtman tried to make a point about the low sales figures for *Two Virgins* in the United States, John quickly corrected him: "Well, it sold as well as Alan Ginsburg [*sic*] or Stockhousen [*sic*] or John Cage, who sell 15,000; these sold about 20 or 30,000, and that you can only compare with other avant-garde works; you cannot compare it with *Imagine*."

Schurtman shifted to the *Wedding Album*, which John described as having "a little singing on it, but I would term it an avant-garde to differentiate it from the other ones. That is another documentary . . . I think it is pretty obvious what it is. It is a wedding album, only we made ours public, instead of keeping it in the house . . . [it] probably sold 50,000. Kids would want to have that as a souvenir."

Schurtman showed John the big photo in the album's box showing he and Yoko in bed surrounded by reporters.

"What image were you trying to convey to your public?" he asked.

"You can see what is over the bed, Peace and Love," John pointed out.

When asked if there was any adverse reaction to the album or the photo, John replied, "I don't think so . . . No, the picture was great." John ended this series of questions when he stated, "No, I don't see why anybody would be annoyed by the album."

This testimony prompted a discussion between Judge Griesa and Schurtman that made it clear, at least to me, that the judge thought little of Schurtman's attempts to prove that John's artistic reputation had been "badly tarnished" by his avant-garde albums.

THE COURT: I will take [adverse reviews of Two Virgins as evidence]. But if you come to grips with this -- you will hear me more -- Mr. Lennon obviously has certain objectives in his artistic productions, and sometimes it takes the form of the *Two Virgins* album, sometimes it takes the form of an Imagine album. But he is able, presumably, to decide what he will do at a given time, whether it is avant-garde or regular rock music, and this all over the years, I assume, builds a cumulative reputation.

But, at least, it is within his control to some extent, and he is able to decide whether he does avant-garde or a nude album or whatever.

•   •   •

Then the problem is when someone else puts out an album, maybe it is in someone's eyes more respectable than the Two Virgins, but that really isn't the point. It is not his doing. A John Cage

might not put out the same kind of music
that Victor Herbert would, but that is
John Cage's business.

Schurtman did not seem to understand that Judge Griesa
was a trained classical musician. He was a deep thinker. He
knew who John Cage was, who Victor Herbert was. Yet
Schurtman continued to argue that John had not suffered any
damages by the release of *Roots*—to no avail!

THE COURT: You are not getting my
point. You can have an artist who may
be a John Cage. He is determined to
be avant-garde, somewhat outrageous.
Now, somebody puts out an album of Victor Herbert [music] and says it is John
Cage. Then it may be a lot more respectable, a lot more, maybe millions of people would like it better than John Cage,
but that would damage John Cage, because
John Cage does not want to be the kind
of a middle of the road, have a middle
America effect. So you can't come in and
say, 'Gee, John, you were improved by
this,' because that is not John Cage's
objective.

●　　●　　●

I think it is just as true in damages. The problem is to come to grips
with what was Mr. Lennon's objective as
to what he was trying to convey to the
public and match that against the image conveyed by the Roots album and the
Roots commercial and see where there

```
are differences and try in some mysteri-
ous way to put a dollar value on it [for
damages].
```

This provided us with clues as to Judge Griesa's views on how John was damaged by the *Roots* album. Unwilling to accept he'd lost that argument, Schurtman shifted gears and argued *Rock 'n' Roll* would not have sold well because the album's songs were not characteristic of Lennon's best-selling music, i.e., original songs.

Amid Schurtman's questions John called the *Rock 'n' Roll* album "a step out of character" for him. But just a step.

"It is characteristic for me to be a bit oddball," he testi-fied, adding that he was known for several things, including his original music and lyrics and old rock and roll songs.

He pointed out that some of The Beatles' biggest hits were old rock and roll songs and that *Live Peace in Toronto* sold well because it was partially an album of a rock and roll revival.

Also, John said, songs that carry the feeling, if not the lyr-ics, of '50s rock are on *Imagine*—"I Don't Wanna be a Soldier Mama" and "Crippled Inside," the latter evoking the classics put out by Sam Phillips at Sun Records where Elvis Presley, Jerry Lee Lewis, Roy Orbison, and Carl Perkins recorded. He gave another example: the hit single from *Walls and Bridges*, "Whatever Gets You Thru the Night," could have been written in the '50s.

He called '50s rock "the biggest influence on my life."

Judge Griesa summed up the issue and the question it raised.

```
    THE COURT: Now I guess one of the
things we are trying to get at, and I
don't know how to find out, is this: If
your fans have grown to enjoy your char-
acteristic music, and buy those records,
then you come along and you record an
```

album which is maybe very fine, but is different; now isn't that going to affect the sales in some way?

THE WITNESS: But, your Honor, it could go either way.

THE COURT: Sure it could.

THE WITNESS: Unfortunately all this happened out of it. OK. So I made the album knowing full well that I was making an album I didn't write. But I made it for a specific reason. I didn't want to write it. I wanted to do something as if I was 15. That was the reason I did it. And it is a good chance it could have gone either way. I might have been taking a risk, sure, and if nobody ever told me, 'Don't do it' -- no record company people said, 'Don't do it, it's a terrible idea' -- I thought it would be a good idea and it would be fun and it could have gone either way. It could have been the biggest seller I ever had and it could have been the lowest seller. There is no way of knowing.

If people knew what would sell we'd all be sitting at the Fontainebleau in Miami, so it is not the same as this. But there is a good chance it could have sold twenty times more. I might have done Volume 3 and 4 if it had gone the other way.

Q   (MR. SCHURTMAN) Or it could have sold a lot less.

THE COURT: How does one find out?

THE WITNESS: Only by putting it out.

John also described what he would have done in terms of radio promotion for *Rock 'n' Roll* absent the illegal release of *Roots*. Capitol would have arranged in-person or telephone interviews with "disc jockeys, station managers, anybody Capitol thinks I should meet. Sometimes it is a station manager like the whole West Coast. There is one guy on the West Coast, one guy on the East Coast. If you see them, you are all right for both coasts. . . . This time for Rock and Roll all I could do is WNEW locally in New York. I didn't have time to go out to the coast and talk to everybody."

With a few more questions, John's cross-examination was over, as was his testimony in this second trial; and there was no need for John to testify in the third trial that would follow this one. He was free!

John Lennon was the best witness I ever represented or put on the stand in my forty-five year career. He was very easy to work with. John rarely forgot anything we discussed. He never let the questioner push him around or intimidate him, but he also never showed obvious anger. Instead he raised his voice and gave a "sharp" answer such as, "I don't live in some ivory tower."

John and Yoko did not enjoy sitting in court listening to testimony, but they did it. Their presence sent a clear message to Judge Griesa: *we care about this case*. I believe John's presence helped when he testified. Listening to the testimony of Morris Levy and his witnesses helped him when he testified because he was very observant. John picked up things very quickly. He listened (even though he might have been writing a song in his head).

There is no way of measuring how John helped determine the successful outcome of Morris Levy's extortionate case.

Chapter 39

Rolling Stone's Dave Marsh

April 1, 1976
US District Court
New York City

HOWARD OBTAINED CRUCIAL TESTIMONY from our next witness, Anthony V. Stevens, the master cutting engineer at the Master Cutting Room.

Stevens used the notes of master cutting engineer Gregg Calbi, who worked with John on *Rock 'n' Roll* in February 1975, to show that the sound level on each track on the album was set at different levels. Each one's settings were done individually, affecting the sound heard when the record was played. Very clear, very simple.

Yet Schurtman raised time-consuming objections to Stevens' testimony. He also objected to Howard referencing the notes used to master *Roots*, written by Levy's master cutting engineer, Joseph Brescio. The judge overruled his objections.

"It is an utter waste of time . . .," the judge said. "I disagree. It is a fact question. Let us go on. We got all this equipment here and we are supposed to hear Mr. Marsh."

Schurtman was deliberately exasperating Judge Griesa. When he falsely claimed he couldn't cross-examine the witness, the judge had had it. Agreeing with him, he ruled: "No cross." He turned to Stevens and said, "You may step down."

Despite Schurtman's bogus objections, Howard proved that *Roots* sounded different from *Rock 'n' Roll*. Why? Because the *Roots* master cutting engineer didn't make any changes to the limits of the settings on any of the *Roots* tracks. This approach meant all the tracks sounded the same. However, when Gregg Calbi worked with John on *Rock 'n' Roll*, they changed the settings on every track until each one sounded how John wanted it to sound.

I then called Dave Marsh, who testified he was an associate editor of *Rolling Stone* magazine, which had a circulation of 450,000 biweekly. He was responsible for its two review sections, record and performance, and his *American Grandstand* column. He testified that for four years he was an editor at *Creem*, the second largest pop music magazine in the United States. He'd also written for *Newsday* on Long Island, the *Real Paper* in Boston, and again for *Newsday* before joining *Rolling Stone*.

Dave testified that he first met John the previous day when he came to court. I questioned him.

> **Q** Now, can you tell us what role John Lennon played in The Beatles music?
>
> **A** Well, he was first of all, with Paul McCartney, the group's principal songwriter and one of its two principal singers with Paul. More than that, I think to many people who were growing up at the time I did, John was in The Beatles the quintessential representative of that sort of '50s rock and roll spirit that as The Beatles' music grew more sophisticated, there was always a danger of losing, and really what made the music most exciting was the tension between the sophistication, on the one hand, and the primitivism, on the other.
>
> I don't mean to imply by that that John's solely a primitive artist, because he is not. But I mean to say by

that that he operates within that kind of artistic tension between sophistication and primitivism. And that was his role in The Beatles as I saw it, it was to substantially introduce that tension from one side or the other.

Q Can you give us an example of a song that Mr. Lennon wrote while he was with The Beatles that you thought was kind of representative of his talent?

A There was a song that was the title song from their movie called "Help," which was a basic rock and roll song with a basic rock and roll lyric. Yet at the same time there was a song, which I believe is John's, that I associate with John, on the same record, called "Ticket To Ride" which introduces a guitar line that I don't know where he got to this day.

And then there are other songs. I mean I can't do it with a single song, because it varied from song to song within the text of the album usually.

There was a song like "Norwegian Wood"[1] basically used some kind of Indian influence to -- and an incredibly complicated lyric that was, I mean it was just the contrivance of the lyric itself is very artistic.

On an album called Rubber Soul, which comes to mind, there is a song, a record called "Strawberry Fields Forever,"

[1] "Norwegian Wood" was on *Rubber Soul*. "Strawberry Fields Forever" was not on *Rubber Soul*. It was released twice in 1967, as a single with "Penny Lane" on the flip side, and again on the *Magical Mystery Tour* album.

which is not so much for any of those things but just for the total effect as a record which John wrote is remarkable in terms of its use of distortion effects and things like that.

Q   Would you say that Mr. Lennon was the most creative member of The Beatles band?

A   I would say that with Paul McCartney he was the most creative member of The Beatles band.

Q   Do you still consider Mr. Lennon an important artist today?

A   Absolutely.

Q   Can you tell us why?

A   Well, I mean, in a way I think John has become a more important artist since he struck out on his solo career and when I say solo career, having witnessed yesterday's testimony, can I describe what I mean from the Plastic Ono Band album?

THE COURT: OK.

A   Plastic Ono Band album came out at a time when many people who had been through the various countercultural trips of the '60's, drugs, sex, politics, rock and roll, were beginning to reflect back on exactly how self-indulgent and perhaps self-destructive they had become. And in very direct terms, the songs on that album discuss one man's journey through that time. That is what the song "The Dream is Over" is about.

THE COURT: What is the song?

THE WITNESS: "The Dream is Over"; I think that was played yesterday.

Q Is that on the Plastic Ono Band?

A Yes, the last track, I think. I could be wrong about that, but as he sings 'I don't believe in God, I don't believe in Jesus, I don't believe in Dylan, I don't believe in The Beatles'; when John Lennon says 'I don't believe in The Beatles,' first of all, it was the first time that anyone had really convinced anyone that The Beatles were not going to come back together again, which was a shock to the young audiences that rely on rock and roll. And I don't mean to dwell on that song too much but really, what John meant to me is what one does after the adolescent dream of rock and roll is over.

And he has done that, I think, in very brave risk-taking ways, and I think the *Imagine* album also is a part of that.

Q What?

A The notion of imagining, being able to imagine a world with no rules or religions or politics or structure.

Q What do you mean by risk-taking?

A I mean taking a chance that he is going to say something (a) that might offend somebody; (b) that might not be understood; (c) that might not be commercial and therefore could affect his career economically. I mean all of those things and I think John has simply done all of those things.

Q Mr. Marsh, I show you Plaintiff's Exhibit 35 which is the John Lennon Rock and Roll album and ask you if you have ever seen that record?

A Yes, I have.

Q Can you describe that album and what, in your opinion, it purports to do?

A It is an album of about a dozen '50s and early '60s rock and roll songs which basically is John Lennon's interpretation of the tradition of the rock and roll tradition out of which his own work has grown.

Q Would you describe it as kind of a musical history?

A It is a musical history, it is again what I call Sergeant Pepper, it is a conceptual album. All of John's records are conceptual in the sense of building around a unified theme.

Q Will you also say that doing that Rock and Roll album was a risky thing for Mr. Lennon to do?

A It was for this reason: the songs that he was doing are considered in the rock and roll community to be classics both in terms of the songs themselves and the performances of the songs.

The first thing he had to tackle in that was the notion of himself as the quintessential rock and roller; secondly, he had to take the chance that he could beat at least one or two of them -- one or two of the greatest songs in the history of rock and roll. That is risk to me. Those two things. I mean he put out -- his reputation as an artist on the line, doing this project. I believe that.

Q Have you ever heard the Rock and Roll album?

A Yes, I have.

Q I show you Plaintiff's Exhibit 34, which is the Roots album, and ask you if you have ever seen that album?

A Yes, I have.

Q Have you ever heard that album?

A Yes.

Q Did I ask you to play both of those albums?

A Yes.

Q So that you could contrast them?

A Yes, you did.

Q Do you recall when that was?

A About, I would guess about three weeks or a month ago, it could have been a little longer, a little less.

Q And you played the two of them?

A Yes, I did.

Q More or less at the same time or one right after the other?

A I played them -- unfortunately I only had one turntable to do it with, but I played them in a track-by-track comparison. I don't mean track one, side one. I mean "Be-Bop-A-Lula," "Be-Bop-A-Lula," in that kind of sequence and I did that, yes. It took me a couple of hours to do it.

Q Because the two albums are in a different sequence?

A Yes, the sequence is different. I didn't want to give the impression that I compared them song by song, I should say.

Q Did you thereafter write me a letter with respect to your comparison of the two albums?

A Yes, I did.

MR. BERGEN: Your Honor, I would like to mark this as Defendant's Exhibit DP.

(Defendant's Exhibit DP marked for identification)

Q Mr. Marsh, I show you Defendant's Exhibit DP and ask you if that is the letter that you wrote to me?

A Sure is.

• • •

Q You have heard both of the albums and you said you compared each song?

A Right. Right. Exactly. I compared the two versions.

Q What is your opinion of the two albums?

A You mean --

Q Comparing them, which is the better of the two albums?

A The Capitol album is the better of the two simply because it seems professionally put together.

Dave's testimony would only get worse for Levy. Put simply, it would fully substantiate John's counterclaims and those of Capitol/EMI.

Chapter 40

"Do You Want Me to Tell You [What I Heard]?"

April 1, 1976
US District Court
New York City

I then asked Dave his opinion of the sound on the *Roots* album.

    A It is shoddy, it is fuzzy. It sounds like those old bootleg records that kids used to make out of cassettes. That is what it sounds like to me.

• • •

    Q Is there surface noise on the *Roots* album?
    A Very much.
    Q Does the surface noise obscure or inhibit any of the instrumental passages?
    A Yes. And I told him that.
    MR. SCHURTMAN: I object to Mr. Bergen's leading his own witness. Either ask him to give an opinion or put the letter in.
    THE COURT: I am sure that Mr. Bergen and this witness have gone over the sub-

stance of the witness' testimony and Mr. Bergen knows that. And it really isn't -- this is your opinion, right, what you are telling us in court?

THE WITNESS: Yes.

THE COURT: It is not Mr. Bergen's opinion.

THE WITNESS: It is what I heard on the record.

THE COURT: All right. Let's go in some efficient way. It is all right with me. Mr. Bergen, go ahead.

Q Can you describe what impact the surface noise in your opinion has on the Roots album and the songs on the Roots album, I should say?

A Well, on any music all the surface noise would get in the way of the music itself. I mean, music is a noise that is made deliberately and surface noise is a noise that is made not deliberately.

In this case it is especially crucial because John is trying to create a specific musical effect, or a series of specific musical effects in order to recreate that specific era.

Q Can you tell us what those specific musical effects are?

A A lot of that has to do with, well, on different tracks there is the different arrangements and stuff, tell their own story. But in general it has to do with -- because the music is so primitive, it needs to be very loud and I think the surface noise inhibits the volume on the record. It should be rough

but those records were recorded crudely
and not -- I mean they were recorded
at a time when the technology was very
crude, but certain parts of them should
be very crisp, for instance, and they
are not.

    Q You are talking about the old rock
and roll songs.

    A I am talking about the old rock
and roll songs.

    Q So in recreating them --

    A In order to recreate them these
things need to be placed in a certain
proportion, a certain perspective, in
relationship to one another and to the
voice.

    THE COURT: I am very sorry. I have an
urgent call. Just give me a second.

    (Recess)

The judge left the bench. I went back to speak with John.

"Are you going to play *Roots* now?" John asked.

"Yes, why?"

"Jay, I can't sit here while it's being played," John replied. "I'm going to leave."

"Leave? You can't leave," I said. "You have to stay here while we play a few of the *Roots* tracks. The judge wants to hear them."

"I don't want to hear the songs," John said. "They're going to sound awful."

"John, you absolutely cannot leave. You have to stay. Judge Griesa will notice that you're not here and that won't look good. Okay?" John looked at me. He didn't reply. He didn't leave.

The recess ended.

    Q Can you tell us, Mr. Marsh, what

the sound on the Roots album lacks?

A It lacks presence. I mean it is not there as fully as it might be. Sort of rock and roll -- old rock and roll was really punchy-like, and this is sort of flattened out. It is not as powerful as it might be. I mean those are the terms that I would describe it in, if I were reviewing it in Rolling Stone and I am just a little worried about the jargon here.

THE COURT: Do what you need to do with this equipment.

MR. BERGEN: I will go to that right now.

THE COURT: I am quite positive this witness will have to come back. If we can get through with the equipment --

[MR. BERGEN]: I am going to play the song "Ain't That a Shame" on the Roots album, Plaintiffs' Exhibit 24, and then after I finish I will ask some more questions of Mr. Marsh.

THE COURT: This is on Roots?

MR. BERGEN: Yes.

THE COURT: Who wrote this?

THE WITNESS: I am not sure. The original was written by A. Domino.

MR. BERGEN: According to the liner notes on the John Lennon Rock and Roll album, "Ain't That a Shame" was written by A. Domino and D. Bartholomew.

(Record played)

Q Now, Mr. Marsh, do you recall the difference between that version of "Ain't That a Shame" and the one that is on the

Rock and Roll album?

MR. SCHURTMAN: Why don't we play it [from the Rock 'n' Roll album]?

MR. BERGEN: I am going to.

THE WITNESS: In making comment about the '50s Rock and Roll, it is not all the same. There are several distinct regional styles. This style of music is called New Orleans Rhythm and Blues, and it is characterized by a shuffle drum pattern, and the horns, both of which are derived from basic New Orleans. On the Roots album, as I remember —

Schurtman must not have bothered to listen to the two albums because he now talked himself into a trap of his own making.

MR. SCHURTMAN: Your Honor, can I suggest before the witness explains the difference, if you hear them both side by side while we still have it in mind?

THE COURT: That is a good thought.

MR. BERGEN: I am playing the same song, "Ain't That a Shame," from the John Lennon Rock and Roll album.

(Record played)

MR. SCHURTMAN: Your Honor, you have heard both songs one after each other in each album. We don't need someone to tell you what you have heard.

THE COURT: I don't. Do you want me to tell you?

MR. SCHURTMAN: Yes.

THE COURT: I don't think there is any comparison. The Rock and Roll is so much

```
clearer; the voice was very poor and in-
distinct on Roots, it was almost hidden
there. I could not tell it was John Len-
non singing or anybody singing; it was a
voice. The elements, whatever they are,
were all fuzzed up in Roots, and I don't
know whether you call it surface noise
or what kind of noise, but it was fuzzy,
and I would not get anything much out of
it. Now, the Rock and Roll, it seems to
me, the voice was clear and distinct,
and every other element was distinct,
and the beat was distinct, and the dif-
ferent things that had very little impact
or any clarity on the Roots album, were
clear and that is that.
     MR. BERGEN: May I play one more?
     THE COURT: I think it speaks for it-
self.
```

In "Sue You, Sue Me Blues," Dave Marsh's *American Grandstand* column in the June 17, 1976 issue of *Rolling Stone*, he describes this amazing moment from his ringside seat on the witness stand: "Schurtman's expression could be compared to a coal miner's who's just heard the first timbers crack."

```
     MR. SCHURTMAN: If those are your
views, they are your views. Why do
you need a witness to keep telling
you what you just heard?
```

Schurtman seemed desperate to get Dave Marsh off the witness stand.

```
     THE COURT: I guess I was the one agi-
tating for a witness, but I had never
```

```
heard that thing on this kind of equip-
ment, with all due respect to my law
clerk's stereo set.
```

Schurtman tried a diversionary tactic, claiming that the Record Plant equipment was the reason that *Rock 'n' Roll* sounded better than *Roots*.

```
THE COURT: Tell me how it sounded
here compared to how it sounded when you
played it before [in your office].
THE WITNESS: Exactly the same.
```

That destroyed Schurtman's claim about the equipment.

```
MR. BERGEN: I will play one more. I
will play "Peggy Sue"² on the John Len-
non Rock and Roll.
(Record played.)
MR. BERGEN: We will play the same
song on the Roots album.
(Record played.)
THE COURT: What style of rock is
that?
THE WITNESS: That was done by a guy
named Buddy Holly, who recorded in New
Mexico with a guy named Norman Petty. It
was called Rock-A-Billy, and it is very,
very similar to the style that John was
referring to as Sun earlier today.
```

[2] In May 1977, after the case was over, Judge Griesa's law clerk, Susan Jackson, asked if I could send her the *Rock 'n' Roll* and *Roots* albums. She explained that his staff wanted to give the albums to the judge at a dinner celebrating his fifth anniversary on the bench since this was his "favorite case." After receiving the albums, she wrote in her thank you letter, "[The judge] became particularly enamored of 'Peggy Sue' during the trial and now he can listen to it to his heart's content."

THE COURT: You described the "Ain't That a Shame" as New Orleans rhythm and blues. The word 'Sun' does not mean anything.

THE WITNESS: Sun was a particular place in Memphis, a particular record company like Capitol, although it's much smaller, where Rock-A-Billy records were played. Rock-A-Billy, as the title indicates, is rock and hillbilly music.

THE COURT: So this is based on hillbilly rather than New Orleans?

THE WITNESS: Based on hillbilly music more than on black music or soul music or rhythm and blues music, as it was called then, but with an element, and Buddy Holly and the Sun people John was talking about this morning relied on the country; the Sun people used more R&B.

THE COURT: Meaning rhythm and blues?

THE WITNESS: Yes.

MR. BERGEN: May I just play one of the two songs that is off [Rock 'n' Roll] that is on the Roots album and that will be the last thing?

THE COURT: Sure.

MR. BERGEN: I am going to play "Angel Baby," one of the two songs on the Roots album that was left off the Rock and Roll album.

(Record played.)

THE COURT: Any further questions?

MR. BERGEN: I have no further questions. [I should have asked Dave to comment on "Angel Baby," but Judge Griesa noticed and corrected my mistake.]

THE COURT: Is there some comment that
should be made on that? I don't know.
Mr. Marsh, could you tell us?
THE WITNESS: Well, first and most obvious, that song is so badly out of tune
that John isn't even singing in the same
key as the band. If you would like my
physical reaction to that, it was because the saxophone is so badly out of
tune. I mean, that is the worst. The
band is also out of tune with John. It
sounds like the kind of thing you hear
in strip, or like one of the strip shows
one sees in the movies.

That's how we ended the day, adjourning to 10:30 a.m.
April 7. All of us, including Dave Marsh, drove uptown.

"Judge Griesa did not like Schurtman's objection to my using Brescio's notes to question Mr. Stevens," Howard said.

"Schurtman was that way with Judge MacMahon, too,"
I replied. "He doesn't seem to understand how annoying and
counterproductive it is to Levy's defense."

"He really likes to jump up and object," said Dave. "Is he
like that every day?"

"Pretty much," I answered.

"Mr. Schurtman is an active objectionable person," said
John, clenching his teeth together and doing his "Mr. Schurtman, I can't hear you" imitation.

"We've been doing impressions of Mr. Schurtman for a
while, Dave," I told him. "We noticed how he talked in January. It's helped us not get infuriated at his interruptions. Right,
John?"

"It has helped," John replied. "One has to try to have a
sense of humor about this mess."

Chapter 41

Even the Vinyl Is Recyled

April 7, 1976
US District Court
New York City

JOHN AND YOKO ARRIVED AT MY OFFICE AT 9:30 A.M., probably
looking forward to the final trial day on the counterclaims.

"Judge Griesa's law clerk called on Monday," I told them.
"She asked if we could bring the sound equipment back for
today's session. I told her I'd arrange for that to be done." I
turned to John.

"Are you glad that we've reached the end of the second part
of the case?"

"I am, we are," replied John. "Yoko and I think this part of
the trial has also gone very well. Dave's testimony has been very
helpful and interesting. He really knows his rock and roll."

"He does and he will not let Schurtman push him around,"
I said. "Dave is very opinionated. He has strong views and is
not afraid to express them directly and in detail. He's taken
some heat from artists and other critics for some of his opin-
ions, but that's okay. I think the judge likes him and will rely
on his testimony."

We talked a while longer before heading to court.

I picked up my questioning of Dave where we'd left off on
April 1. We focused on "Angel Baby" and "Be My Baby," two
songs that appeared only on the *Roots* album.

    Q Would you say that both of these

versions, "Angel Baby" and "Be My Baby," would be embarrassing to Lennon's reputation as an artist?

A   Extremely.

Q   Why?

A   Well, first of all, I mean just on the basic level of sheer competence, in the same way that I wouldn't want an article of mine in which I had misspelled words and used bad grammar being distributed to the public, that would be an embarrassment to any creative person, that their work -- that their worst and least competent work should be displayed before the public, that would be embarrassing. Secondly it is embarrassing because of the association the song has with his career and its associations with Spector's career and Lennon has always [been] one of the principal champions of Spector.

Q   Is the order -- on a rock and roll album is the order on the tracks important? In other words, which track follows which one?

A   I think it is important on any record, so it certainly is there.

Q   And the order of the tracks on the Rock and Roll album and the Roots album are different, aren't they?

A   Substantially different, yes.

Q   And in your opinion does that make a difference in terms of the complete thing?

A   It makes a difference in the way that the album flows. Can I take a look at the two albums?

Q I am handing you Plaintiffs' Exhibit 35, which is the Rock and Roll Album, and Plaintiffs' Exhibit 34, the Roots album.

THE COURT: Mr. Bergen, I know we have had this before, but is it correct that "Angel Baby" and "Be My Baby" are the only two songs that were included in the Roots that aren't included in Rock and Roll?

MR. BERGEN: That's right, your Honor.

A I don't think there is any great deal of difference. There might be some -- again, I haven't heard these records in several weeks, maybe a month, but there is a difference in the way the two records flow, but it is real hard for me to judge because those two out of tune tracks come up in the middle of these sides and that disrupts the thing as much as anything.

Q Are any of the things that you have testified about with respect to the Roots album true of the Rock and Roll album? In other words, the quality, the sound?

A No. I mean the quality on the [Rock and Roll] album is a very well engineered album, it is a very well produced album. Regardless of the quality of any of Mr. Lennon's interpretation, which is even more subject to taste than that.

THE COURT: Wait a minute. What are you saying?

THE WITNESS: I am saying the basic quality, the competence of the production, the engineering, and the pressing --

THE COURT: On which album?

THE WITNESS: On the Rock and Roll album. I find none of the problems I have mentioned here.

Q Now, what is your opinion of the effect [of] the Roots album on Mr. Lennon's reputation as an artist?

A Were it widely distributed I think that the effect could be potentially devastating. Since The Beatles also had broken up his force commercially had been splintered. He had gained and lost through a series of projects and the public is very -- I mean it is a very [volatile] public. Some Time in New York City he got political and the rock community tends by and large to mistrust people who are overtly political. He had been going through the whole immigration thing. People were very confused about what the status of his career was and the word was sort of out well maybe some of all this legal trouble and Beatles trouble and one thing and another has sort of cost him his talent. And I think to come out with something like "Angel Baby" or "Be My Baby" in a package like that, which looks like not only -- I mean to me, as a rock fan what it would look like is not only doesn't he know how any more but he doesn't care any more, he can't even cover up for himself.

Q Are you talking about those songs or the total package?

A I am talking about the total package from the cover on in.

When I questioned Dave about the *Roots* cover, he raised several interesting issues.

Q Mr. Marsh, I show you Plaintiffs' Exhibit 34, which is the record jacket of the Roots album. Now, would you comment with respect to the credits on the back of the album?

A It is unheard of for an artist to credit himself as the singer or performer after every track. This John Lennon (indicating), that space is always used, when it is used, to indicate the author of the track. I think that could be really confusing, or, again, embarrassing to John Lennon. It makes it look as though he wrote "Rip It Up." Everybody knows he did not write that song on here, "Sweet Little Sixteen," that Chuck Berry wrote it.

Q You say because John Lennon's name appears after each track on the Roots album there would be confusion that people would think that Mr. Lennon was trying to say that he wrote the songs?

A I am saying that there is that possibility, and given that we are dealing in part with an audience who [doesn't] know about the '50s music because they simply were not around then, it is possible to mislead them, and then

if they found out if they had been misled or thought they had been misled --

THE COURT: There is no indication of
the composer or author on here.

THE WITNESS: No, that struck me as
strange, too, because rock and roll is
the writer's medium and you give credit
to the man who wrote the song.

THE COURT: What would the normal
credit be? What would be said here?

THE WITNESS: Well, in the case of
"Sweet Little Sixteen," which is a song
and I know the author of it, this would
say "Sweet Little Sixteen," Chuck Berry.

MR. BERGEN: Maybe I can show him Exhibit 35, the Rock and Roll album.

Q Explain to the Court in a little
more detail what you mean?

A Well, it is the standard form of
citation for all the songs written by
one person. Generally at the bottom it
would say All Songs by John Lennon,
Copyright, and whatever, and the publishing company. Here if you would like
to look at this, this shows the author
of the songs, the publishing company,
the performance rights, and the tracks,
a convenience for the radio or air play.

Q You are referring now to the Rock
and Roll album?

A To the citations after the titles
on the back.

MR. SCHURTMAN: What is the relevance
of radio play?

THE WITNESS: I was trying to explain
why the various bits of information are

given.

THE COURT: Do we have the right word here? Is Chuck Berry the composer or writer or author or what do you call him?

THE WITNESS: The songwriter.

•   •   •

Q   Now, looking at the [Roots] cover itself, Mr. Marsh?

A   Front?

Q   The front cover, can you comment with respect to the cover?

A   People just don't do covers like that. I mean, because I know something about journalism and printing, I am aware that this picture is not from an original photograph. I mean, the colors are nothing less than garish. It looks thrown together.

Q   Were The Beatles a group known for having interesting covers on the albums?

A   Yes, one of the first groups in rock and roll to sort of raise album covers to the point where design societies now publish books about album cover art, and The Beatles really initiated that.

•   •   •

Q   Handing you the two record albums, can you comment on the vinyl on the records themselves, the vinyl that the record is made of?

A I will have to compare them. Well, you should perhaps see for yourself, your Honor, but as with the copies that I compared in my office, the Rock and Roll is shinier, which generally would indicate that it is made from virgin vinyl, which is to say not recycled vinyl, and it is much less brittle, which is, again some kind of test of quality control in the actual production of the disc itself.

Q Can you also comment, Mr. Marsh, about the advertising for other albums on the back of the record, the *Roots* record?

A Well, again, it just contributes, you know, to the idea that -- I mean it just further destroys the credibility of the project. I mean it is not done. I mean there is a sort of protocol, a sort of good form, bad form situation that is, you know, ethic or something that is developed and you just don't do that. This was done before The Beatles -- something like this might have been done by a record company with the artists of their albums. They might have said "Other albums by Chuck Berry available on Chess records are," and it might have shown the covers very small like this, but it certainly -- I mean people like pictures of artists and such, and they would really expect some kind of esthetic continuity from someone like John Lennon. I would. I do.

Q Do you recall hearing about the

Roots album when it first came out?

A Yes.

• • •

Q Did you hear generally in the industry that there was confusion as to the Roots album?

A I remember asking people questions. The situation was cloudy in my mind until the coverage of the first trial.

MR. SCHURTMAN: I object to the testimony about he asked a couple of unidentified people.

THE COURT: I don't think this is hearsay. Here is one man connected with his business, and he says what he did and heard.

MR. SCHURTMAN: My objection is to the looseness of the testimony -- well, I talked to a couple of people. Who are the couple of people that he talked to, when, and where?

THE COURT: If you want him to be more specific, fine.

Q Do you recall who you spoke to?

A I talked to -- the one person I remember for certain talking to is a friend of mine who lives in California named Greil Marcus who is also a music critic who writes for the Village Voice and Rolling Stone. He is a big John Lennon fan. I remember it coming up in a conversation, and I walked away from that conversation as confused. Maybe he knew but I didn't understand. That's the one I remember for certain. Possibly also with my friend John Landau.

Q Who is Mr. Landau?

A The records editor of Rolling Stone before me.

Q He is a rock music critic?

A Yes, and a record producer.

Q Mr. Marsh, I show you Plaintiffs' Exhibit 201, which is the Rolling Stone issue of May 22, 1975. I ask you if you have ever read the review by John Landau of the Rock and Roll album?

A Several times.

Q Do you agree with Mr. Landau's criticism of the Rock and Roll album?

A In part.

MR. SCHURTMAN: I object to this as irrelevant.

THE COURT: Overruled.

Q Can you tell us how you disagree with Mr. Landau?

A Can I just scan this?

(Pause)

How I disagree?

MR. BERGEN: Yes.

• • •

THE WITNESS: I don't want to go into detail by saying this song is good, that song is good. To me, as a person a couple of years younger and didn't ex-perience the originals of some of these songs quite as directly as John did, John Landau did, John Lennon did, that some of the songs seem much more admirable to me, and in terms of the tone this review seemed much more successful to me than it did to him. He doesn't mention, for instance, "Peggy Sue" and "Stand By Me." I don't think he mentions "Peggy Sue," which to me, I think they are great, right up there with anything John ever did. That's what I disagree with about the review.

MR. BERGEN: I have no further questions of Mr. Marsh. . . .

Chapter 42

A Fascinating Career

April 7, 1976
US District Court
New York City

THOUGH ARGUMENTATIVE, SCHURTMAN'S cross-examination of Dave didn't damage any of his direct testimony. I'll point out some highlights, particularly a period when Judge Griesa questioned Dave, eliciting helpful testimony supporting John's counterclaims.

After Schurtman had been questioning Dave about negative reviews of John's album, Judge Griesa stepped in.

> THE COURT: You said a minute ago, I think that you thought some of the songs on Rock and Roll were successful and some were not so successful, something like that.
>
> THE WITNESS: Some of the interpretation of the songs. That would be clearer.
>
> THE COURT: Whatever you meant to say.
>
> THE WITNESS: That is what I mean.
>
> THE COURT: Let me just start again. What would your evaluation then be of the Rock and Roll album? Spell it out in as much detail as you wish.
>
> THE WITNESS: It is a mixed success to

me artistically, because I think Lennon overreaches. I don't think the two Chuck Berry songs, "Sweet Little Sixteen" and "You Can't Catch Me," are done in a way that to me expands their emotional meaning or historical significance or make it clear to me why Lennon would choose to do them in such a way. On the other hand, "Stand By Me" and "Peggy Sue" did exactly that, expand the songs emotionally.

THE COURT: The Berry songs are which?

THE WITNESS: "You Can't Catch Me" and "Sweet Little Sixteen."

THE COURT: Now, then, the two others that you mentioned --

THE WITNESS: "Peggy Sue" and "Stand By Me" are very difficult songs.

THE COURT: What do they do?

THE WITNESS: I think they expand -- I am speaking in terms of comparing Lennon's to the original -- they expand the feeling in new ways, and to really feel John Lennon's affection for those songs and the people who made them and they helped shape his art in new ways.

THE COURT: Any other comments on the album generally or on individual songs?

THE WITNESS: I think the album in terms of the song selections -- and there are many reasons offered for that here -- I think the song selection is overly conservative. I think that John picked relatively obvious songs. Had he been able to come up with acceptable versions of "Angel Baby" and "Be

My Baby," had those songs been properly
performed, my judgment would be signifi-
cantly altered.

THE COURT: Read the last answer.

(Answer read)

THE COURT: Do you know enough about
the sales of this type of album to give
me an opinion as to whether these fac-
tors would affect the sale of the album?

• • •

THE WITNESS: It is clear to me that
an artist has a basic quality and after
he has been around and established a career, he has a basic audience that buys
pretty much everything he does that is
meant to be a commercial record.

THE COURT: Now, go ahead.

THE WITNESS: If he comes up with
something that is really exceptional,
and it can only be exceptional in terms
of the fact that it is exceptionally
useful to be played on a radio and at-
tract people in this way more than ordinary, then he will sell more records.
I don't think that artistic questions
are directly felt by consumers, and I
think it is borne out by my experience
as a reviewer or critic, that readers do
not really agree with us as a group, and
that some of the most widely panned sell
the most records, to judge from their
trade charts. Now, talking about these
reviews by Marcus and Landau, there is
a grain of truth in them for people who

are utterly crazy about John Lennon,
real John Lennon fans. Both Marcus and
Landau are that more than myself. But
the mail that we got from Lennon fans
when our review came out -- when did the
Rolling Stone review come out? In March?

MR. BERGEN: It was in May, I think.

THE COURT: Wait. Let us get it.

MR. LARSON [Capitol/EMI's attorney]:
May 22.

THE WITNESS: I remember at that time
being impressed by the amount of reader
response we got from that and how favorable to the album it was, how people
were saying this is a great record, the
people who write letters. Now, that is
my basic contact with the rock consumer.
What I am trying to say is, I think the
reasons why rock records sell -- some
do and some don't for better or worse
-- given the minimal standard of quality
and the lack of alienated content, is
pretty mysterious to everyone concerned.
But I do think if John had come up with
a hit single on that record, he obviously would have sold more records, and
the way to come out with a hit single,
my argument to him, the way you come up
with a hit single is to choose a song
you don't hear every day.

•   •   •

THE COURT: You mentioned a couple of
times radio. Now, what is the importance
of radio? What happens with a new re-

cord, usually?

THE WITNESS: What happens with a new record on radio?

THE COURT: Yes? Is radio so important?

THE WITNESS: Radio is a crucial factor in selling records.

THE COURT: What usually happens on radio with a new album?

THE WITNESS: With an artist of John Lennon's stature?

THE COURT: Yes.

THE WITNESS: It gets played like crazy. You are going to hear it, depending on the album and how accessible it is to radio people, if it is not political, about Attica -- you are going to hear it as much as once an hour or at least a couple of times a day in the first week or two.

•   •   •

It would affect the sales. What would have affected the sales in a positive way in my opinion is if Lennon had done things that he didn't do -- I mean, I don't know how to prove a negative; I don't know how to prove that if he had managed to come up with -- and I am not suggesting that he should have put out that version of "Angel Baby" or that version of "Be My Baby" -- but if he had come up with songs that are strange, that the ordinary person would not put on there, then I think, yes, it would

have been more attractive, because it
would have the element of surprise and
the idea that you are getting a treat, I
mean, on the purely most emotional kind
of thoughtless level.

This exchange ended Judge Griesa's questioning of Dave.
Schurtman resumed his cross-examination.

Q When Mr. Bergen questioned you,
Mr. Marsh, you started to give us a his-
tory of The Beatles and the world of
rock and roll and then you told us about
Mr. Lennon. Was that your opinion of Mr.
Lennon's career since 1969?
A You mean since the break up of The
Beatles?
Q Right. Since he's been a solo art-
ist.
A In an artistic sense?
Q In any sense.
A I mean artistically I would con-
sider at least until he started spending
a lot of time in this immigration thing
I would consider it one of the most
brilliant careers in music, and even
since then it's been a fascinating ca-
reer artistically speaking.
THE COURT: What time do you fix for
the immigration problem?
THE WITNESS: Around right after --
around the same time as the Some Time in
New York City album. I mean right after
that or right before that.
Q Would you say that his career
since leaving The Beatles has been a

confused one?

    MR. MCHUGH [Apple Records' attorney]: Objection.

    THE COURT: Overruled.

    A It isn't confusing to me. I guess it depends on how much attention you pay to it.

    Q Would you say Mr. Lennon has been having career difficulties since he left The Beatles?

    A Not since he left The Beatles but since the immigration.

Schurtman's cross-examination stopped shortly after this. Dave was excused with a thank you from Judge Griesa. Court then adjourned until 2:15 p.m.

When we were all in the limo, I turned to John and Yoko.

"Nothing interesting is going to happen this afternoon," I said, "and the need for any testimony from you is over, John. When court resumes I'm going to tell the judge that we rest our case. He'll probably ask to hear the entire *Rock 'n' Roll* album. He's mentioned that several times. I can tell by the look on your face that you're not interested in sitting through that. So, we can have lunch and then you can go home or you can go home now. Up to you."

"We'll go home now," John replied. "We've spent enough time in court. I miss spending time with Sean, taking care of him. We can give Dave a ride uptown. Thank you, Jay and Howard. You did a great job on the counterclaims."

"You're welcome," I said. "And thank you both for being in court every day.

"Dave, thank you for your help," I added. "Your testimony was invaluable. I hope you had some fun and got some material for a column or two."

"It was great," Dave said. "Very interesting to watch the testimony and how Judge Griesa ran the trial. It was also interesting being an actual witness. I won't soon forget the experience. Please let me know how this turns out."

"I certainly will," I replied. "We'll probably know what the judge's plan is before we adjourn this afternoon. I'll call you, John, with an update."

Howard and I got out of the limo and watched them drive away.

Court resumed at 2:15 p.m.

"John Lennon rests," I informed Judge Griesa.

Since we had the equipment in the courtroom and the judge had some time, he requested that I play him some of John's songs, specifically select ones from *Walls and Bridges* and the entire *Rock 'n' Roll* album.

When we finished he thanked me and said, "I think we can let the equipment go back."

After a short recess Mr. Schurtman read some excerpts from deposition testimony as part of his defense on John's counterclaims.

Judge Griesa informed us we'd have oral argument on the Capitol/EMI and Lennon counterclaims at 1:30 p.m. the next day. Then we adjourned for the day.

When we returned to the office, I called John to tell him about the oral argument.

"Jay, Yoko and I would rather not come to court tomorrow," John said. "We've seen and heard enough from Schurtman. It's over as far as I'm concerned. We won the first trial and you told me that the judge is going to award damages on the counterclaims. I think I've made my point with Morris Levy. I don't want to listen to any more of Schurtman's nonsense."

"I understand," I said. "It's not going to make a difference one way or the other to what will happen tomorrow. We're starting at 1:30. I'll call you when I return to the office."

Chapter 43

Victory Again

April 8, 1976
US District Court
New York City

PRETTYMAN STARTED ORAL ARGUMENTS ON BEHALF of
Capitol/EMI's counterclaims. He explained that Capitol
would have permitted sales of *Walls and Bridges* to continue
and waited until March or April to release *John Lennon Rock 'n'
Roll.* Instead, pressured by Levy illegally releasing *Roots*, Capitol released *Rock 'n' Roll* as quickly as possible.

Capitol was forced to reduce its usual $6.98 price per
album to $5.98 because *Roots* was priced at $4.98.

On February 8 Capitol's situation worsened when Adam
VIII began airing TV ads for the *Roots* album. Prettyman
argued that the ad campaign, which ran until February 16, confused John's fans and the general public. When *Rock 'n' Roll* was
released on February 13, its potential buyers weren't sure which
of the two albums was the official one. The *Roots* TV campaign
had gotten the jump on Capitol. The albums were competing
against each other.

Testimony by Capitol executives and John supported
Capitol's argument that *Rock 'n' Roll* had been rushed into final
production and release. Evidence proved that normal national
radio promotion was missing except for one interview John did
with Scott Muni in New York. The inventive TV commercial
that John had planned never happened. A weaker version was
launched well after *Rock 'n' Roll* was on sale.

Capitol could not release a single from *Rock 'n' Roll*, a pivotal promotional step. The single would have generated radio airplay and word-of-mouth advertising for the album.

Various other Capitol promotional steps, such as T-shirts, posters, and in-store displays, either never happened or arrived too late to really boost sales and engage the public's interest.

Judge Griesa found in his February 20 decision that Morris Levy didn't have a contract with John Lennon that permitted him to release *Roots*—and knew that he didn't. Therefore, his deliberate violation of John's rights, and Capitol's, created the scenario Prettyman outlined for Judge Griesa.

Prettyman's final argument demonstrated that *Rock 'n' Roll* sold fewer albums than it would have absent the illegal *Roots* album. According to Capitol's projections, *Rock 'n' Roll* would have sold 750,000 albums.

I then presented John's contentions: he lost royalties because of reduced sales and the reduced album price, both due to the illegal *Roots*. Once Judge Griesa determined Capitol's damages, he would mathematically calculate John's losses.

We had requested at least $50,000 for damages caused by the illegal use of John's name and likeness on the shoddy *Roots* album cover and TV ads. John also sought compensation for damage to his artistic reputation. Not only did Levy use the unfinished "rough mix" 7-1/2 ips tapes John gave him for listening purposes only, but he included the inferior "Angel Baby" and "Be My Baby." For legitimate artistic reasons, John removed both from *Rock 'n' Roll*.

I argued that "brings you to the fact that the *Roots* album itself was of very poor quality and that it was embarrassing to Mr. Lennon and damaging to his reputation. Anyone listening to the album can tell that. And I submit that Mr. Levy and Big Seven and Adam VIII not only should have known that it was of poor quality, but must have known it. Yet they still released the album."

Additionally, I argued that the Lennon and Capitol telegrams warned Levy he had no right to release *Roots* when he knew John Lennon was exclusively signed to Capitol/EMI. Levy then commenced two bogus lawsuits, which wasted court time and resulted in substantial unnecessary legal fees and expenses.

It was then Schurtman's turn. He had earlier given Judge Griesa a lengthy legal brief, admitting during his presentation that "the better part of my brief is devoted to [causation] ..."

Simply stated, Schurtman's main argument—practically his sole argument—was that the illegal release of the pirated *Roots* album, supported by nine days of national TV advertising, had absolutely nothing to do with the premature and rushed release of *Rock 'n' Roll*. Given the evidence presented at the January trial, the judge's February 20 decision, and the evidence just presented, this was an absurd defense. The evidence was overwhelmingly favorable to John and Capitol/EMI.

"I am a little distressed to hear from your Honor's remarks that you seem to have, at least in principle, accepted [Capitol/EMI's and John Lennon's] views of causation ... ," Schurtman told the judge. "I now have an uphill battle to convince your Honor that, in the first place, [Capitol/EMI and Lennon] did not sustain any losses, and, in the second place, even if they did sustain losses, these were not proximately caused by our torts."

"Mr. Schurtman, let us not have an uphill battle," Judge Griesa replied. "I told you that I would be an idiot if I sat through the [January trial and six days now] and didn't think ..."

Later Schurtman's "uphill battle" became an avalanche when he elicited anger from the judge.

"I think what happened here, your Honor, ... is that when this situation with Levy arose Capitol decided that they were out to get Levy and teach him a lesson. They decided not to go for an injunction because they didn't think they had a strong enough case for an injunction, they so testified. They decided to kill Levy in two ways: by sending the telegrams and trying to get him off the air and cutting off his suppliers, and by killing him in the marketplace."

This assertion was a total misrepresentation of the evidence we presented! But Schurtman was not finished.

"This was an economic decision," he said. "It was not a necessary consequence of what Levy did. They regarded him as a pirate and they were out to get him by whatever means they could, including by what I could only refer to as predatory pricing, cutting the price below the normal wholesale and retail prices. They figured if the price is cut low enough they will demolish Levy and teach everyone else a lesson."

> THE COURT: What is predatory about a price of $1 above [Levy's] price?
>
> MR. SCHURTMAN: It isn't, your Honor. [An admission by Schurtman.]
>
> THE COURT: There isn't anything in the record about such a motivation. That's really fantastic.

> •   •   •

> THE COURT: You don't have to go back over that. This thing about motivation to kill Levy -- . . . Stick to the evidence. I think we can go on to the next point.

Schurtman's argument went on and on to the point where even he said, "I know I am repeating myself. . . ." The judge interrupted him.

"Yes, you are, really," Judge Griesa said. "You have no idea how much I have thought about this. I think the other lawyers have gone through this rather quickly, and that is about all we can do. We have been on this case for days and days and days."

When Schurtman implied that the judge was "prepared to award several hundreds of thousands of dollars without going through the detailed transcript in the case . . . ," Judge Griesa put Schurtman down.

"I will tend to my business," he told Schurtman, "and you tend to yours."

Still making his lack of causation argument, Schurtman stated, " . . . I implore, your Honor, I have worked day and night . . . till four o'clock this morning getting the brief into final shape—at least your Honor will take a look at it. That is all. That is my request to you."

The judge stopped him—again.

"Mr. Schurtman," he said, "I can assure you that I am quite familiar with the record. I have pored over the record quite a bit. I appreciate your brief. I think it has been helpful in focusing on points as we go along. But I want to put my decision on the record here and now because I feel I am best able to do it now, rather than wait."

Pursuant to federal law, Judge Griesa stated that "[t]he following statement constitutes my findings of fact and conclusions of law." His opinion covered twenty-five trial transcript pages. He found that "Levy had absolutely no basis for believing that he had the legal ability to issue this album, and I cannot in all realism believe that he had even thought he had such right."

In other words, Morris Levy never truly thought he and John had made an agreement on October 8, 1974. He deliberately released *Roots*, knowing he had no right to do so, and he commenced two lawsuits, knowing that his claims were fraudulent. It was a classic Morris Levy grift, one of his sleazy con jobs—gambling that John and Capitol/EMI would make a deal with him. He'd been pulling illegal scams on singer/songwriters and recording artists for years, but he finally met his match in John Lennon. Determined to erase Morris Levy from his life, John stood up for his rights and won. It was a lesson I have remembered to this day.

The judge also found that the illegal *Roots* was the direct cause of the damages suffered by Capitol/EMI and John, flatly rejecting Schurtman's lack of causation argument.

To summarize the damages awarded against Levy and Adam VIII:

$122,000	to Capitol for lost profits on sales of 100,000 additional units of *John Lennon Rock 'n' Roll* but for the competing *Roots* album
$105,000	to Capitol for lost profits caused by the album price reduction from $6.98 to $5.98
$ 10,000	to Capitol in punitive damages for the deliberate unauthorized release of *Roots*
$ 27,500	to EMI for the pressing fee on the 100,000 lost sales of *John Lennon Rock 'n' Roll*
$ 10,000	to EMI in punitive damages for the deliberate unauthorized release of *Roots*
$274,500	**Total to Capitol and EMI**
$ 66,000	to John Lennon for lost royalties on sales of 100,000 additional units of *John Lennon Rock 'n' Roll* but for the competing *Roots* album
$ 43,700	to John Lennon for lost royalties caused by the album price reduction from $6.98 to $5.98
$109,700	**Total damages to John Lennon for lost royalties**
$35,000	to John Lennon for violation of his rights under Section 51 of the New York Civil Rights Law
$10,000	to John Lennon in punitive damages for the deliberate unauthorized release of *Roots*
$154,700	**Total to John Lennon**
$429,200	**Total to Capitol, EMI, and John Lennon**

In awarding the $35,000 in damages to John for the unauthorized use of his name and likeness and reputational damage,

Judge Griesa added a telling comment:

> I wish to add on this point that
> there has been a great deal of evidence
> produced in the record as to the exact
> status and movement of Lennon's career.
> I am convinced of the fact that Lennon
> perhaps has a career whose balance is
> somewhat more delicate than the career
> of other artists. Lennon has attempted
> a variety of ventures both in popular
> music and avant-garde music. Lennon's
> product tends to be somewhat more intel-
> lectual than the product of other art-
> ists. What this means in my view is that
> Lennon's reputation and his standing are
> a delicate matter and that any unlawful
> interference with Lennon in the way that
> Levy and the Roots album accomplished
> must be taken seriously. Consequently, I
> award the damages that I award.

The hearing ended with this strong affirmation of John's reputation and standing as an artist.

Howard and I thought the damages award would be substantial but we were beyond delighted with the actual amounts! [For a case of this type in 1976, the damages were very significant when compared to today's standards.]

Back in the office, I called John. I explained that Judge Griesa read his decision after the oral argument, awarding Capitol/EMI $274,500 and him $154,700.

I expected John to be delighted. Instead he complained that the $154,700 wouldn't even cover his legal fees.

"What are you talking about?" I said. "I don't know anything about your legal fees. You're David's client. He's responsible for sending invoices to you, not me. I don't see those invoices. You've said many times that 'business' is not your job. It's not mine, either. My job was to be your lawyer on the Levy case.

"You and Yoko also had said many times you just wanted to 'hold down' the amount of money you'd owe Morris Levy. You don't owe him anything. Judge Griesa dismissed his bogus breach of contract claim. Now Morris owes you $154,700—a great result!"

We rambled on about what a mess it would've been if we'd lost the breach of contract claim and he and Capitol/EMI had been forced to pay damages or make a deal with Levy.

"John, you're completely free of Morris Levy," I said. "You accomplished your goal."

"I'll speak to David about the fees," he replied. I suspected Yoko would have that conversation.

"I'll send you the opinion," I said. "I think you'll enjoy reading it, especially the last three pages. The judge said a number of very complimentary things about you and your career. He stated that your product is, and I'm quoting, 'somewhat more intellectual than the product of other artists.' Judge Griesa had great respect for you artistically and personally. You should appreciate that."

I told John the trial on Levy's next claim—that Big Seven would have earned hundreds of thousands of dollars in royalties if he had recorded "Angel Baby"—would begin the following week.

"You don't have to be there," I said.

"Good," he replied. "I don't want to be involved anymore."

"That's okay. Schurtman will have a very difficult time proving lost publishing royalties. Levy's claim of hundreds of thousands of dollars is wildly exaggerated."

John thanked me and we said goodbye.

Judge Griesa's decision meant that Levy was a liar and a fool again. His bullying had failed spectacularly. He'd spent his career in the music industry cheating artists. Everybody in the industry knew this. Many executives, artists, managers feared him. His underhanded methods and Mafia connections were well known.[3]

Yet John Lennon had shut him down. The defeat was a major embarrassment for Levy.

The next day I sent the judge's opinion to John. I did not expect to hear from him.

John's direct role in the Big Seven case ended on April 7, 1976. He had made it clear that he was finished with Morris Levy. He'd told me how determined he was to be a full-time parent to Sean. It seemed like that's what he would do. I hadn't been prepared for that personally after such a long, tough haul working together, but I understood.

The final part of Levy's shakedown was scheduled to start in six days.

---

[3] Levy's power in the music industry was never quite the same after the case. In 1986, a federal investigation into organized crime's involvement in the record business led to a 117-count New Jersey indictment of seventeen individuals charging numerous crimes by mobster Gaetano "Corky" Vastola's New Jersey criminal organization. Levy, his accountant, Howard Fisher, and Dominick Canterino, allegedly a member of Vincent "The Chin" Gigante's Genovese crime family, were indicted on extortion charges. They were convicted in 1988 on two counts of conspiracy to extort, but the trial judge threw out Fisher's conviction for lack of evidence. Levy was sentenced to ten years in prison and fined $200,000. He lost his appeal. Two months before he was to begin his prison sentence in 1990, he died of colon cancer. He was sixty-two years old.

Chapter 44

Value of Unrecorded "Angel Baby"

April 14, 15 and 26, 1976
US District Court
New York City

BIG SEVEN (AND SCHURTMAN) WERE STILL CLAIMING that John's album *Walls and Bridges* was the "next" album under the October 1973 "Come Together" settlement agreement. Obviously, it was not.

Big Seven alleged that John had recorded only two Big Seven songs—"Ya Ya" and "You Can't Catch Me"—on *Rock 'n' Roll*. It was seeking damages for John's failure to record one song—either "Angel Baby" or another Big Seven song.

In January Morris Levy had testified that the monetary value of future music publishing royalties resulting from John Lennon recording a Big Seven song would be "[m]any hundreds of thousands of dollars." He claimed that if John had recorded "Angel Baby," other artists would "cover" that song by recording it, earning Big Seven more publishing royalties.

Schurtman called several witnesses, some of them music publishers. Their testimony actually proved that it was extremely difficult to calculate the dollar value of John recording a Big Seven song.

Judge Griesa asked one of them, "if you heard a group of songs, you couldn't predict which ones would earn a lot and which ones would earn a little, right?" The witness answered: "No. If somebody could, they would get millions." The witness was also unfamiliar with "Angel Baby" or its artists, Rosie and the Originals. It became painfully obvious that Schurtman had not carefully prepared his witnesses' testimony.

In a last ditch effort to salvage Big Seven's claim, one publisher testified that if Stephen Stills, "[a] very well known artist," had recorded "You Can't Catch Me" *after* Lennon's recording, the value of the copyright would have been enhanced.

Schurtman then stated "that the *Rock 'n' Roll* album came out in February, 1975, and Mr. Stills *recorded* his cover record [of "You Can't Catch Me"] in January, 1976." (emphasis added) I was unfamiliar with Stephen Stills' recording of "You Can't Catch Me." The next day I found *Stephen Stills Live* at Colony Records. When I removed the cellophane wrapper, I thought, *Bingo!* Printed on top of the record's sleeve were the words: "*RECORDED LIVE MARCH 8 & 9, 1974* AT THE AUDITORIUM THEATRE IN CHICAGO." (emphasis added) It was recorded almost a year *before Rock 'n' Roll* was released! Stephen Stills' "You Can't Catch Me" was *not* a cover record of John Lennon's recording.

Irwin Robinson was *our* music publisher witness. In response to Judge Griesa's questioning, Robinson testified:

> . . . 'Angel Baby' in my estimation
> is not a song that will fit very many
> artists in the future, it won't become
> more fitting to artists because it was
> recorded by John Lennon . . . the origi-
> nal record [of 'Angel Baby'] by Rosie
> and the Originals was a hit record in my
> opinion because of its sound and the na-
> ture of the artist and the time in which
> it was released.

This testimony, unrebutted by Schurtman, proved that if John had recorded "Angel Baby" on *Rock 'n' Roll*, the probability of cover versions would be negligible, if not zero.

I later called Levy back to the witness stand. He made one

damaging admission after another, proving that neither he, Big Seven nor Schurtman knew anything about Stephen Stills' "You Can't Catch Me" recording, proving that Schurtman's claim that it had been recorded in "January, 1976" was false.

Levy's testimony demolished Schurtman's claim that Stephen Stills' 1974 live version of "You Can't Catch Me" was the result of John Lennon's recording the song on 1975's *Rock 'n' Roll*.

Morris Levy and William Schurtman had been humiliated again! I wished that John had been there that day. We would have had some great laughs in the limo on the way uptown.

Big Seven and John Lennon rested. Judge Griesa told us his office would call to set a date for final arguments.

Chapter 45

Levy's Pyrrhic Victory

May 28, 1976
US District Court
New York City

SCHURTMAN DIDN'T BOTHER TO APPEAR for the May 28 oral argument. Kanzer stood in for him.

Over three trial days and eight witnesses' testimony totalling 427 trial transcript pages, Judge Griesa's July 13, 1976 opinion awarded Big Seven only $6,795 in damages!

He ruled that John "breached the Come Together Settlement agreement [by] failing to include a third Big Seven song in the 'Rock 'N' Roll'"album."Therefore, Big Seven was "entitled to a mechanical royalty at the rate of 2 [cents] per album" on the "so-called 'domestic' sales of 'Rock 'N' Roll' [of 342,000 albums]." After deducting the writer's share of the mechanical royalties in the US and for foreign sales (plus other foreign deductions), the judge arrived at the $6,795 figure.

Judge Griesa ruled:

```
    I conclude that the phrase "next
album" in the Come Together Settlement
Agreement referred to the rock and roll
album, and that it was in that album
that Lennon was obligated to include the
three Big Seven songs.
```

The judge also stated that "Big Seven formulated [an]

additional theory as relating to 'cover records' by artists other than Lennon, which would have yielded additional royalties" because John's recording would "increase the popularity of the song and stimulate other artists to record it." He ruled, however, that "Big Seven's evidence turned out to have certain fatal defects, the most important of which" was:

> The only witness who specifically at-
> tempted to analyze "Angel Baby" was an
> expert witness who testified for Lennon.
> This witness testified that "Angel Baby"
> was not the kind of a song which was
> likely to give rise to numerous cover
> records even after a recording by an
> artist such as Lennon. This witness tes-
> tified that, to the extent "Angel Baby"
> achieved popularity, this was largely
> due to the type of <u>sound</u> produced by the
> recording artists.

Finally, Judge Griesa highlighted another flaw in Big Seven's "additional theory":

> . . . the defense proved that Stephen
> Stills' recording of "You Can't Catch
> Me" was made in March 1974, before the
> release of Lennon's album, although the
> actual release of the Stills recording
> was not made until January 1976 for cer-
> tain apparent administrative reasons. In
> any event, the Stephen Stills recording
> of "You Can't Catch Me" was not a cover
> record stimulated by Lennon's recording
> of that song.

Morris Levy's claim of "[m]any hundreds of thousands of

dollars" in royalties if John had recorded another Big Seven song was another Levy "pipe dream." Not even close. The negative results of Levy's bogus lawsuits gave new meaning to the word "failure."

I had the July 13 decision delivered to John but did not hear from him.

On July 27, 1976, John was granted permanent US residence and given his coveted green card. He was free of legal responsibilities. So Sean, then almost ten months old, was his sole responsibility. As Bob Gruen described it years later in his excellent book, *John Lennon: The New York Years*, John was in his "househusband period."

The August 10, 1976 final judgment decreed that Big Seven and Adam VIII's claims against John, Capitol/EMI, Harold Seider, and Apple Records, Inc. were dismissed. It awarded $419,800 in damages against Morris Levy and Adam VIII, Ltd.—$274,500 in favor of Capitol/EMI and $145,300 in favor of John. (The parties had agreed to reduce John's award of $109,700 in lost royalties by $9,400 to $100,300.) Big Seven was awarded $6,795 in damages against John.

The clock began running for Morris Levy, Big Seven, and Adam VIII to file an appeal to the Second Circuit Court of Appeals.

Prettyman stunned me when he called to tell me that Capitol/EMI were settling with Morris Levy and Adam VIII, Ltd. for $170,000 payable over two years with a down payment of approximately $20,000. He also said Kanzer had told him that Levy had "no intention" of making a settlement offer to John. Kanzer had demanded that Prettyman not tell me the settlement amount, but Prettyman had refused to do so.

I could not understand why Capitol/EMI would cut John loose after the enormous artistic and financial success he and The Beatles had generated for them since 1962 and would continue to generate in the future.

I immediately sent a letter to John explaining that Capitol/EMI had gone behind our backs and negotiated a settlement with Levy. I told him that the burden was now entirely on us to defend Judge Griesa's favorable decisions. I explained that Levy was again trying to put him on the defensive and make us come to him with an offer to avoid opposing Levy's appeal. In other words, he was still trying to bully John.

This tactic did not change John's determination to be rid of Morris Levy forever.

On January 11, 1977, I delivered to John our appellate brief opposing the two briefs filed by Adam VIII and Morris Levy. Levy had hired another law firm to represent him personally on the appeal. I invited John and Yoko to the Court of Appeals oral argument on January 27.

Chapter 46

Levy Loses Vindictive Appeal

January 27, 1977
US Court of Appeals
New York City

JOHN CALLED ME A FEW DAYS BEFORE the oral argument. Although we hadn't spoken in some time, our conversation was as if no time had passed. He wanted to check on the oral argument date. We arranged for John and Yoko to pick up Howard and me on Thursday morning.

The Second Circuit courtroom is on the seventeenth floor in the same courthouse on Foley Square where we had tried the case. The Second Circuit and the D.C. Circuit in Washington are the two most important appellate federal courts in the US, after the Supreme Court.

The courtroom is the largest in the thirty-seven-story tower, proportioned at 66 feet long, 33 feet wide, with a ceiling 22 feet high. It has beautiful brown wood paneling and several tall windows on the left facing north. As one enters the courtroom, there are rows of wooden benches on either side of a center aisle. A low railing with a gate in the middle separates the spectators' seating from an area where attorneys can await their cases being called. At the front of this area is a podium with a table and three chairs on either side; that's where attorneys arguing an appeal sit.

The bench where the usual three-judge panel sits is at the end of the room on a platform raised above the floor. In the middle of the wall behind the judges is a door through which they enter. Below the bench are tables and chairs for court clerks, a court reporter who transcribes the oral arguments, and other court personnel.

The three-judge panel that day was comprised of Circuit Judges Anderson, Oakes, and Gurfein.

When we entered the room we sat in the back row. I sat next to John and Yoko. As the other oral arguments began, I noticed Yoko had a deck of tarot cards in her hands. She was shuffling them and turning them over. I knew nothing about tarot cards. *Yoko's swami's prediction last January turned out great for us*, I thought. *Here's hoping she gets a good reading.*

The Second Circuit's three-judge panels are known as a "hot bench," meaning the judges, with the assistance of their law clerks, have carefully read the parties' briefs and are well prepared to question the respective attorneys closely.

The oral argument that day was typical. During my presentation two of the judges questioned me in detail about Judge Griesa's award of damages to John for lost royalties. Griesa's calculation had been based on Capitol's reduced price for *Rock 'n' Roll* and his projection that an additional 100,000 albums would have been sold but for the release of the illegal *Roots* album.

I'd been puzzled by a question one of the judges posed to me about *Live Peace In Toronto*. I hadn't played the B-side of that album. On our way uptown after the argument, I asked John, "What's on the B-side of *Live Peace In Toronto*?"

"Oh, that was just Yoko moaning and screaming," he replied, as Yoko sat beside him.

When we arrived at our office, we shook hands. I told John I'd call when we got a decision.

On April 13, the Court of Appeals issued its eleven-page opinion. Written by Circuit Judge Oakes, it began as follows:

```
"Everybody's hustlin' for a buck and
a dime
    I'll scratch your back and you
```

```
scratch mine
    All I can tell you is it's all show
biz. . . . "
    The words of John Lennon above are an
appropriate introduction to this case,
which involves alleged broken promises
and acrimony between supposed friends in
the recording industry.[1]
    _____

[1] J Lennon, "Nobody Loves You (When
You're Down and Out)" (1973), recorded
on the album "Walls and Bridges."
```

The judges unanimously affirmed Judge Griesa's dismissal of Big Seven and Adam VIII's breach of contract claim and the $6,795 award to Big Seven against John. They also affirmed the $35,000 award to John for injury to his reputation in violation of his rights under Section 51 of the New York Civil Rights Law. However, they ruled that Judge Griesa's finding that *Rock 'n' Roll* would have sold 100,000 more albums but for the unauthorized release of *Roots* was erroneous, thereby reducing the award for John's lost royalties to $49,912.96. They also reversed the $10,000 punitive damages award to him. The total damages award to John was $84,912.96, less $6,795.

I called John, who answered the phone. I told him we'd won but that the court had reduced his damages by about $60,000. He was disappointed at the reduction but happy that Judge Griesa's other findings had been affirmed. He was also glad the case was finally over and he was truly rid of Morris Levy.

John congratulated us on the victory and thanked me for our help. I sent him the opinion on April 20.

My journey with John Lennon was over. We had moved the case to a trial in record-breaking time—ten months. John had stood his ground. We'd stopped Morris Levy's attempted extortion.

Chapter 47

"The Dream Is [Really] Over"[4]

December 8, 1980
The Dakota
New York City

AFTER DEFEATING MORRIS LEVY, John was finally free of the drama of the music business, the endless legal battles, the rumors and gossip. Released from the snares of fame, he was free to simply be John Lennon, New Yorker, husband, and father—something he'd longed for, as he'd often told me. That was the person I came to know, beginning in February 1975. John had won more than a hard-fought court battle. He'd won his right to live his life the way he wanted to.

I wouldn't be the person I am today if I hadn't met John and spent time with him, if I hadn't gotten to know the man behind the persona. He touched my life in ways that left me changed. For the better. Without realizing it, I began wanting to live my life the way I wanted to, not the way someone else wanted me to. That connection with John put me on a road that began to change my future.

In addition to my litigation practice, I began to develop a rock and roll/entertainment law practice in 1977. I reached out to a number of people in the music industry who I'd met through working with John.

In 1978 Jimmy Iovine, the engineer who worked on *Rock 'n' Roll*, introduced me to a Brooklyn band named Flame. Jimmy had just produced their first album, *Queen of the Neigh-*

[4] John Lennon, "God," recorded 1970, *John Lennon/Plastic Ono Band* album.

borhood, on RCA Records.

Capitol Records referred Eve Moon to me. Eve, a singer-songwriter and excellent guitarist, had begun her career singing on the streets of Greenwich Village. I negotiated her recording agreement with Capitol in 1980. That same year, Record Plant became my client. Eve would record her first album there.

On the evening of December 3, 1980, when I entered Record Plant, I was surprised to see Yoko Ono sitting on a couch at the far end of the room. I walked towards her.

"What are you doing here?" she asked before I even had a chance to say hello. I explained that a client, Eve Moon, was recording an album for Capitol Records there.

"How's John?" I asked, assuming he was working in one of the other studios. Yoko didn't answer. I wish I had asked her what studio he was in so I could say hello! I didn't.

After visiting with Eve, I headed out and said goodbye to Yoko. "Please give my best to John," I added.

Five nights later, I was awakened at 11:40 p.m. by the telephone on my night table. I answered.

"Jay, turn on the TV," I heard a friend say. "John Lennon's been shot."

Johnny Carson's *Tonight Show* had been interrupted. A reporter for WNBC Channel 4 was standing outside Saint Luke's Hospital on the Upper West Side, recounting how John had been shot earlier in front of the Dakota and was dead on arrival. I was in a daze, still half asleep, now in shock. I turned off the TV. After a few minutes, I had to talk to someone else who knew John.

I called Jimmy Iovine who was producing a Tom Petty and The Heartbreakers album in LA. When he picked up, I told him the news of John's death.

"Oh my God," he said before the line went silent. I didn't call back. Although we knew each other well, Jimmy and I never mentioned John's death or that call again.

The next morning, devastated and numb, I caught my usual 7:30 a.m. bus to the City. I was sleepwalking. I bought a card for Yoko and Sean. At my office colleagues tiptoed around me in an awkward, unspoken acknowledgement of how much I'd grown to care for John. I was uncomfortable, didn't know what to do with myself, but knew I had to do something. Focusing on work was out of the question.

My only thought was to go where I could feel John's presence. I grabbed the card, left the office, and headed toward the Dakota. I passed places where John and I had walked together. I didn't linger to reminisce. I felt an urgency to be where John had last spoken, breathed, laughed, where he had most recently been alive.

The Dakota was still blocks away when I heard the noise of a large crowd. I may have even broken into a run until I was stopped by a massive crowd filling Central Park West and Seventy-Second Street. It stretched for blocks, mourners come to pay their respects.

I shook my head at how naive I had been. Had I really thought I could just go up to the Dakota, walk under the archway entrance, and leave a card with the doorman?

I stood for a few minutes as I was pushed deeper into the crowd. Out of the hundreds of signs being held in the air, the one I most remember, perhaps because it best echoed my own feelings, simply read "WHY?"

EPILOGUE

Walking back to the East Side, my thoughts turned to
a few nights earlier, when I saw Yoko sitting on the couch. I
knew John was in one of the studios. Yet I didn't ask her which
studio. I know he would have been happy to see me. We would
have given each other a hearty handshake, maybe a hug. We
had bonded during the course of our time together. He was
delighted we'd been victorious over a bullying, threatening
Mafia associate.

I'll always regret not speaking up, not asking Yoko, "What
studio is John in? I want to say hello." I passed up this opportunity to give him a smile, a thumbs-up, anything to show how
much I missed him and our walks and talks.

Big Seven v. Lennon had opened up new vistas for both of
us. John had chosen to fight a battle on many fronts. I was at
the center of a very important case for John. He emphasized
that by attending twenty days of the trial with Yoko. He was
facing multimillion dollar damage claims. His reputation as a
preeminent singer/songwriter, performer and activist was under
scrutiny because he was linked to Morris Levy, a gangster, by
Levy's bogus claims! Finally, at issue was John's overall artistic
integrity because he was standing up to a music industry grifter
who regularly cheated artists, which was unheard of.

John's stunning tragic death on December 8, 1980, acceler-
ated my process of personal change.

On February 15, 1981, I found *my* voice. I spoke up in a
way I rarely did before; and that began an exploration of my
life on February 28. While there were setbacks along the way,

with help, I gradually found new levels of peace and happiness. It took years and sadly caused me to lose vital life connections. It's a never ending process.

When I began rereading John's trial testimony, I knew I had an as yet-unwritten chapter in his life to tell that the world might appreciate. He gave so much of himself through his music and artistry. I thought, this story that he and I had lived together could be illuminating and a comfort to his fans, to his followers, to the millions of hearts he has touched. Yes, the pages in those boxes contained the story of an exciting trial with fascinating John Lennon testimony, funny stories, and insights into the 1970s rock and roll world—a court case John had planned to one day tell about in song. And they contained the story of a quiet, peaceful, happy time in John's short, artistically influential life.

As the late Tom Petty said in a 1983 interview, "I was glad that John Lennon could be happy for a few years. If that made people nervous, so what?" [5]

As I stood in that crowd outside the Dakota that sad December morning, I realized I was just one of many who felt a personal connection to the genius that was John Lennon—except that I actually knew him in person. With his gentle spirit, his intelligence and humor and, above all, his work to "give peace a chance" and end violence and suffering on planet Earth, he holds a special place in all our hearts. Perhaps that is the beauty of his legacy. We all remember him as someone who gave, and continues to give, unique witness and voice to the struggles and triumphs of his—and our—human experience.

We can only Imagine what further greatness he would have achieved had he survived and continued his spirited dialogue of love and friendship with us all. Today's world could certainly use his guidance and wisdom now.

[5] Charles M. Young, "Tom Petty Is Sorta Like God And Sorta Like The Rest Of Us, And Other Theological Insights," *Musician*, March 1983, 9.

Acknowledgments

MY WIFE, DIANNE ARBOUR, has been the love of my life for almost twenty-five years. Over the past four-plus years I've been working on this book, she has been a constant source of love, support, helpful criticism, encouragement, laughter, and wisdom. I could not have completed this project without her by my side.

This book never would have been written absent the friendship, guidance, and experience of the late Dale M. Jacobs, MD. Dale was a one-off. I am eternally grateful for his presence when I was in need.

When I began writing and researching in April 2017, I discussed my project many times with my close friend, playwright/director Catherine Gillet. In September Catherine told me that she and Marianne Carruth, executive director of the Tryon (NC) Fine Arts Center, decided I should do a live multi-media show entitled JOHN LENNON, the MOBSTER & the LAWYER. Catherine helped edit my script and shape the show, along with Michelle Newman, our technical director. We performed the show seven times between March 2018 and February 2020 to enthusiastic audiences. Catherine also has helped many times with suggestions for the book manuscript and as a regular booster of my morale.

Lorraine Ash, my memoir mentor and collaborator, edited and finalized the book manuscript over the past two-plus years. A memoir expert, teacher, author, and editor of *Corona City: Voices from an Epicenter,* Lorraine has been a constant presence and invaluable source of encouragement and supervision as the writing and rewriting has progressed. Her husband, William Ash, has been the irreplaceable formatter/organizer of various drafts and the final manuscript. I cannot thank them both enough.

My longtime friend, Barbara Gilford, author of *Heart Songs: A Holocaust Memoir,* has offered much valuable advice. She introduced me to Lorraine Ash.

In August 2018, via a blind email to the website of Morgan Neville, producer/director of the acclaimed documentary, *20 Feet from Stardom*, I met Robert Gordon, Neville's coauthor and codirector on the 2015 Emmy Award-winning documentary, *Best of Enemies*. A lifelong resident of Memphis, Tennessee, Robert is an author, documentary filmmaker, and expert on Southern music and blues. Since our first email exchange, he has been a wonderful friend and advisor in many subsequent emails and phone conversations. Robert's advice and encouragement have been an important contribution to this project.

David W. Sussman and I have been close friends since 1980. He has provided me with valuable legal and practical advice and encouragement. Thank you, David.

Bob Gruen's friendship and wonderful photographs have been an important contribution to our show and the book. I very much appreciate his Foreword. Richelle DeLora, Bob's license and studio manager, has always been helpful.

Author and good friend, Fred Waitzkin, has been a continuing source of excellent advice and encouragement throughout my entire writing process. Thank you, Fred,

I have also been fortunate to have had support, assistance, and advice from John Ryder, Jim Keltner, Edward Mottau, Max Weinberg, Carol Miller, Michael Lindsay-Hogg, May Pang, Robert Cass, Maura Wogan, Megan Riegel, Kelly Byers, Lindsey Whitfield, Ryan Thackray, Eric Olsen, Mark Pitman, Jay Baer, Ben Dickinson, Lee Christopher Smith, Will Blythe, Larisa Gelman, Rick Kurnit, Robin Rue, Erica Silverman, Mel Parker, Benjamin F. Needell, and my U.K. mate, Paul Sherlock, the best Official Liverpool Beatles Guide.

Wallace Lightsey has been very helpful with copyright questions and other legal matters. Wallace and his wife, Marsha, were responsible for Catherine Gillet, Michelle Newman, and I performing LENNON, the MOBSTER & the LAWYER as the keynote address at the Annual Meeting of the South Carolina Chapter of the American College of Trial Lawyers at The Montage, Palmetto Bluffs, South Carolina, in early February 2020.

Much appreciation goes to my relatives, friends and all others who have encouraged me throughout the several years I have been writing this book.

Finally, almost last but not least my gratitude to my publisher, Tom Graves of Devault Graves Books. I cannot thank Tom enough for seeing in my book the story I've wanted to tell for years and agreeing to bring it to the attention of John Lennon and Beatles fans and fans the world over of rock 'n' roll. Tom quickly realized the importance of the story told herein. We've made a great team working together to accomplish the goal of publication!

Special thank you to Judge Ronnie Abrams for permitting me to use a portion of her interview of Judge Thomas P. Griesa and to Magistrate Judge Stewart Aaron, my former law partner and good friend, for introducing me to Judge Abrams. They are judges sitting on the United States District Court, Southern District of New York.

ABOUT THE AUTHOR

JAY BERGEN WAS A TRIAL LAWYER IN NEW YORK CITY for forty-five years. He has handled antitrust, securities, entertainment, and copyright/trademark cases.

In addition to representing John Lennon, he represented Albert Grossman, Bob Dylan's first manager, in litigation between the two, as well as Terry Knight, founder and manager of Grand Funk Railroad, in litigation between Knight and the band. He assisted 'Til Tuesday, with Aimee Mann, and Face To Face in securing record deals. He represented the Cincinnati Reds, Cleveland Indians, San Francisco Giants, and New York Yankees in Major League Baseball salary arbitrations with the clubs' players. He will not be writing a book about his experiences representing the late George M. Steinbrenner, legendary former owner of the Yankees, although he could!

He lives near Saluda in the Blue Ridge Mountains of southwestern North Carolina.

Other Books in

THE GREAT MUSIC BOOK SERIES

Crossroads:
The Life and Afterlife of Blues Legend Robert Johnson
by Tom Graves

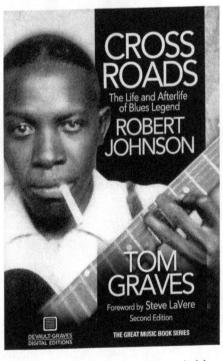

This second edition of the award-winning *Crossroads* by Tom Graves is the author-approved new manuscript that contains updated information and new photographs related to blues legend Robert Johnson. *Crossroads* won the Keeping the Blues Alive Award in Literature in 2010 from the prestigious Blues Foundation and is considered the definitive word on its enigmatic subject.

The result of careful and meticulous research, this stylishly-written biography of infamous blues musician Robert Johnson reveals the real story behind the mythical talent that made him a musical legend. Available in print, ebook, and audiobook, read by the author himself.

318

Timekeeper:
My Life in Rhythm
by Howard Grimes with Preston Lauterbach

Timekeeper is the first-person insider account of the birth and expansion of the Memphis Sound, told by Howard Grimes, the celebrated house drummer from the early days at both iconic Memphis soul studios, Stax Records and Hi Records. Author Howard Grimes backed Rufus and Carla Thomas, William Bell, Willie Mitchell, Ann Peebles, and Al

Green among countless others, and shares his story of artistic and personal tragedies and triumphs in his raw and authentic voice. He was a member of the Mar-Keys and sat in the number one drummer's chair for the Hi Rhythm Section.

Howard Grimes' co-author is Preston Lauterbach, the highly-acclaimed author of *The Chitlin' Circuit, Beale Street Dynasty*, and *Brother Robert* (about the life of bluesman Robert Johnson). With Lauterbach's help, *Timekeeper* is more than a waltz through the past; it is a rollicking, boots-on-the-ground up close look at the rise and ultimate fall of the soul era of Memphis music.

Available in print and ebook.

Sun Records: An Oral History
by John Floyd

Rock 'n' roll was created in tiny Sun Records in Memphis, Tennessee, by owner Sam Phillips, who introduced the world to Elvis, Johnny Cash, Jerry Lee Lewis, Rufus Thomas, Carl Perkins, and many others.

Brush up on your knowledge of Sun's legendary performers by purchasing a copy of *Sun Records: An Oral History* from Devault Graves Books..

You'll be treated to the voices of the pillars of Sun, the artists, producers and engineers who made the place tick. *Sun Records: An Oral History* by author John Floyd is available in print and ebook formats.

Women of Motown: An Oral History
by Susan Whitall

The second edition of *Women of Motown* by author Susan
Whitall contains new chapters and information, updating this
critically-acclaimed oral history of the ladies who made Motown
a sound heard round the world. Originally published to glowing
reviews in 1998, the first edition has long been out of print and
sought after by collectors. Devault Graves Books now brings
the public a new updated edition that tells the Motown story

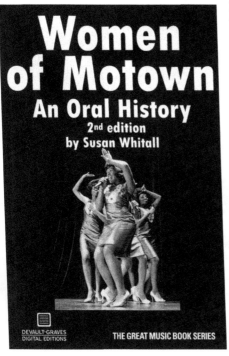

from its beginnings with
Mable John through
the great girl groups
such as Martha and the
Vandellas and ending
with the last iteration of
the glorious Supremes
after Diana Ross left
for superstar status.
Author Susan Whitall,
an esteemed music
writer who is a native of
Detroit, expertly inter-
viewed virtually all the
women who made Mo-
town explode on the hit
charts and lets them tell
their stories in all their
humor, dishy detail, and
the glory of lives spent
recording and singing some of the greatest songs ever written.

Fans of Motown will not want to miss this chance for the
girls to let their hair down and lay it on the line. The stories
are not only fun and exciting, but give a history of a remarkable
company that took African American music from Detroit's
housing projects to the White House.

That's All Right, Mama
by Gerald Duff

Did Elvis' identical twin, Jesse Garon Presley, really die at birth?

Not according to Lance Lee, the hero of Gerald Duff's darkly comic dissection of fame and rock 'n' roll.

Lee, who makes his living as an Elvis imitator, claims to be the long-presumed dead twin. In a style that faithfully reproduces Elvis' plaintive bravado, Lance-Jesse recounts being hidden away and passed off as Elvis' "cousin" until he needs to impersonate Elvis to stave off bullies at school; later, he is obliged to "play Elvis" every time The King has an attack of nerves.

As performing substitute, Jesse has had a lifetime to enjoy being a good-timing, honey-loving, non-drug-dependent Elvis.

DEVAULT
GRAVES

BOOKS